Knowing Godlove Ngufor for years, I can understand why he wrote this masterpiece.

This Book will challenge you to move beyond your level of intimidation, damnation, Isolation, resignation and stagnation to reach your level of elevation and the reason of your Creation.

Don't read this book in one sitting, but digest it and apply it or you won't get the results you want.

D. Landry Fokam Author of 'Rewards of Thanksgiving"

There is no one more equipped to write, Empowering Potential, Rebirthing the African Entrepreneurial Spirit than Godlove Ngufor. He has seen the heartbreak of Africans letting go of their dream, believing in a false hope or just giving up. At the same time Godlove knows the other side—the potential, the hope, and the wealth that is available.

In this book, he not only addresses the biggest thing that holds us back but exhorts us with the responsibility we have and the limited time to go with our God-given potential. Whether you are an African or not, this book holds each of us accountable and speaks to the heart, soul and spirit.

Linda A Olson author of 'Uncovering the Champion Within'

Dear Elodie,

May you fulfil your divine potential. You are a great blessing. Thank you so much

God love.

EMPOWERING POTENTIAL

RE-BIRTHING THE AFRICAN ENTREPRENEURIAL SPIRIT

GODLOVE NGUFOR

Empowering Potential: Re-birthing the African Entrepreneurial Spirit

Bible quotes are from
King James Version (KJV)
King James Version 2000
The Amplified Bible (AMP)
New International Version (NIV)
New Living Translation (NLT)
International Standard Version (ISV)
English Standard Version (ESV)
Scriptures have been underlined for emphasis.
Pronouns used for God and Jesus are capitalized.

DISCLAIMER
The advice contained in this material might not be suitable for everyone. The author designed this information to present his opinion about the subject matter. The reader must carefully examine all aspects of any business decision before committing himself or herself. The author particularly disclaims any liabilities, loss or risk taken by individuals who directly or indirectly act on the information contained herein. The author believes the advice presented here is sound, but readers cannot hold him responsible for either the actions they take or the result of those actions.

DEDICATION

I dedicate this book to my Dad, Ngufor Martin. Thank you so much for bringing us up and being both a mum and dad to us, especially after mum's passing on. With your limited resources, you made the most out of it to take care of us. You have been a great visionary and long before I became closely acquainted with the scriptures; you taught me that "without a vision, there is neither hope nor motivation for living." At the age of 81, you built yet another house, even though struggling with your sight and movement. Your example has helped to greatly empower potential in me.

May God continue to bless and strengthen you as you inspire many through your good example. Even as you turned 82 this year, you have shared with me a new vision to plant flowers around the church in Nyen. May God give you the strength to bring that to fruition and leave yet another legacy.

You are my hero and I love you very much.

CONTENTS

ACKNOWLEDGMENTS

Time and space is inadequate to list the host of individuals that have inspired and helped me to put this book together.

Thanks to Dave and Dorcas Willows. I appreciate your love, encouragement and your constant desire to see me fulfil my divine destiny. May the Lord continue to bless you.

Much thanks to Dr. Ngufor George and Mary Kofo for all your prayers for me. The Lord richly bless and keep you.

I want to thank Pastor Olumide Emmanuel for inspiring me and teaching me aspects of multiple streams of income and financial freedom.

I want to thank Pastors Mel and Heather Mullen for your spiritual covering.

A big thank you to Pastors Grant and Bernie Rogers for your love and prayers.

Much thanks to Peter J. Daniels. Even though I have not met you personally, I have been incredibly blessed by your wisdom over the years.

Thanks to Myles Munroe for bringing to light different aspects of empowering and maximizing potential.

Much thanks to Kathleen Mailer for obeying her divine mandate to teach people to write and publish books.

My deep appreciation goes to Marilyn MacKinnon for helping in editing this book. Your suggestions were very helpful.

I thank all my sponsors for your financial contribution towards the publishing of this book.

Thanks to all my siblings, relatives and friends for all you have invested in me over the years.

I am eternally thankful to my best friend and lover, my wife Glory, for your love, support and for standing by me during this period of sacrifice. Thank you also for helping out with the editing of this book. I would not have been able to write this book without your constant encouragement.

Finally, I give all the glory to the Father of all flesh, by whom all the family in heaven and on earth are named and for sending Jesus to die for my sins to the intent that I might attain my greatest potential both in time and eternity.

FOREWORD

This book is a tool in the hands of the believer and the African to revisit the God given potential in you. We have all been created by a God of great visions and each one of us has been endowed with great potential. The problem is that many people rarely explore their God-given potential and live a life of mediocrity. As a result, they lose their blessings and in the process prevent society from benefiting from their contributions. One of the biggest setbacks of the believer and the African believer in particular is rising up from the miry clay of societal setbacks, cultural backdrops and historical failure in order to fulfill divine destiny. There seem to be a mountain of opposition to overcome in order to attain greatness. Most of these setbacks I believe are in the mind. We must therefore renew our minds and think and speak as God will want us to.

The bible says: I beseech you therefore brethren, by the mercies of God, that you present your bodies a living sacrifice, holy, acceptable to God, which is your reasonable service. And do not be conformed to this world, but be transformed by the renewing of your mind, that you may prove what is that good and acceptable and perfect will of God (Romans 12:1- 2 NKJV).

I believe this book is a resource to the believer of all nationalities and generations. I believe it would be of specific value to the African believer scattered all over the diaspora. Godlove Ngufor revisits the very root of the issues that keep Africans from reaching their full potential and draws answers and solutions from the Word of God. I have no doubt in my mind that this book is a valuable resource in the hands of the reader and that your life will never be the same again as you read prayerfully and meditate on what you read as well as apply the timeless principles in this book.

Adalbert Tanyi

Minister of the Word and Author of "Foundational Principles of Christianity."

INTRODUCTION

Have you ever wondered if things could ever be better in your life? Have you ever wondered why some people seem so blessed and may be you are not so blessed? Have you wondered if your financial situation will ever change? Have you ever asked yourself what happened to the grandiose dreams and aspirations you once had as a child? Are you doing something now in your life or find yourself at a job you hate doing but feel you have no choice and may be do not even see the way out? Have you resigned to mediocrity and come to believe that things will never change, no matter what you do? Have you come to believe like a friend of mine once believed, that the scripture "...the poor you will have with you always", (Mathew 26:11) was written with him in mind?

The answers to these and more are in this reference guide to breathing life into, building and expanding the African Entre-preneurial Spirit!

The first part of this book deals with empowering potential. Everyone owes it to God and to themselves to attain their full potential and fulfil their mission and purpose on earth. A man will never truly be fulfilled without connecting to God, finding out their purpose and attaining his full potential to achieve that purpose.

A lot of people attain a certain level of their potential and become satisfied. However, one day they would come to the realization that they could have achieved more, had they connected with God, found out their purpose and worked extremely hard through His Grace to fulfil it.

History is saturated with stories of people who have jumped and touched the sky of their fields of expertise. People who have been the envy of their generation, only to hear that these same people have committed suicide because of depression. People stand appalled and disillusioned and the media scream the headlines of their decease.

Unless a person is actively empowering their potential, targeted towards fulfilling their God given purpose and in a vibrant relationship with God, frustration would kick in at some point and they will echo King Solomon's words *"Ah, vanity of vanities, all is vanity"(Ecslesiates 1:2)*.

In the second section of this book, the African is encouraged to re-birth the entrepreneurial spirit. I zoom in on Africans because, like everyone, God has endowed Africans with so much potential but they have allowed these potentials go untapped and unused for many decades and centuries.

Long before the advent of colonization, the vast majority of Africans were entrepreneurs in their own rights. Most Africans were traders, farmers, hunters, wine tappers etc. The arrival of the colonial masters popularized the concept of jobs as a more guaranteed and secured means of income.

The argument was that business is too risky. The colonial masters encouraged Africans to abandon their businesses and settle for jobs. Africans became cooks, gardeners, chauffeurs etc., with a guaranteed salary or wage. Eventually, the African was encouraged to go to school and university to get qualifications and credentials that would lead to a job.

But what the African did not learn was that to reach your full potential, a person has to go to the school of capacity building and personal development. University degrees have their place. Most degrees prepare people to become employees and not employers.

JOB as an acronym has two meanings: **J**ust **O**ver **B**roke or **J**ourney **O**n your way to being **B**roke. Starting out with a job is ok, however, most people go to job motivated by pay alone and not by work that brings fulfilment.

This section seeks to argue the importance of being an entrepreneur and developing investment mentality.

It is my prayer that this book will inspire you to rise up and build your capacity and become the leader God has called you to be as you fulfil your purpose in this life.

Godlove Ngufor

SECTION
1

1

OUR FINEST HOUR

Winston Churchill, the revered English statesman, literary genius, and one of the key players in the defeat of Hitler in World War II, is one of the greatest men of the twentieth century. He took the helm of the British government as prime minister in a time of war. In preparation for war, he delivered his famous speech before the House of Commons on June 18, 1940, which has come to be titled by historians as the *finest hour* speech. With unwavering resolve, he justified the reasons Britain needed to go to war against Hitler, who sought to bring the whole of Europe under German domination. Churchill said that Britain's victory would come to be known as the finest hour of the British Empire.

I am convinced that God allows every individual to be born at a particular time so as to empower their potential, fulfil their divine destiny, and make a profound, positive impact in their world.

From one man he made all the nations, that they should inhabit the whole earth; and he marked out their appointed times in history and the boundaries of their lands (Acts 17:26 NIV).

We can decipher from the Scripture above that God has set the bounds of each individual, when and where we should be born and by which parents. However, in the period of time allotted to us, it is our responsibility to cooperate with God so He can fulfil His plans in us and through us. This way, when history is written it can be said "This was their finest hour."

A couple of years ago, when I was a student in Germany, I knew a wonderful Christian brother of fine character. I became acquainted with him through the Cameroon Christian Abroad Outreach (CCAO), a Christian association formed in Germany to help sponsor the preaching of the gospel in Cameroon in the early

2000s.

One day, I got a call from my long-time bosom friend, Edwin, informing me that this brother had passed on. He was walking on the street when he collapsed and died of a heart-related condition. I was confused, startled, and devastated, because he was a young man in his twenties, full of dreams and potential. More so, he was soon to be married to his fiancée, who had just come from Cameroon, his country of origin.

But the most intriguing part of the story is that, when his meditation book was found, they noticed he had recorded something very interesting a few days prior to his passing on. He wrote that he'd had this dream in which he was playing soccer in a field when he was taken off the pitch and replaced by someone else, so he sat in the crowd and watched the rest of the game from the stands. After I heard that story, I recalled the passage in Hebrews.

Wherefore seeing we also are compassed about with so great a <u>cloud of witnesses</u>, let us lay aside every weight, and the sin which doth so easily beset us, and let us run with patience the race that is set before us,

Looking unto Jesus the author and finisher of our faith; who for the joy that was set before him endured the cross, despising the shame, and is sat down at the right hand of the throne of God (Hebrew 12:1-2 KJV).

Hebrews 11 enumerated the giants in the hall of faith and their accomplishments. The writer of Hebrews says that now they are all part of a cloud of witnesses. They were taken off the field of play, which is this life (just like Philemon), and put on the grandstand. One day, you and I, too, will be taken off the field and put on the grandstand.

Until that time comes, we must realize that this is our finest hour, and we must make maximum use of it. We must give it our best shot. I thank God for Abraham, I thank God for Isaac, and I thank

God for all the patriarchs in the Bible. I thank God for all the great leaders, like Winston Churchill, Abraham Lincoln, George Washington, Benjamin Franklin, Martin Luther King Jr., Martin Luther, Mahatma Gandhi, and William Wilberforce, just to name a few. They impacted the world in the different ages in which they lived, through their exemplary achievements. I thank God for all the wonderful women of faith who have interceded for nations, who trained and raised up great world changers. I thank God for those obscure people who did wonderful things behind the scenes, great things that never came to the spotlight, that no one ever knew about and were never on a television screen, except the television screens of heaven.

But we must understand that with respect to the moment, they are immaterial. This is *our* time. We, too, must do our part and leave a legacy. We must rise up and change the world for many generations for the glory of God. We must make our own lasting contribution before we exit the scene. We must brace ourselves against all odds, win many for Jesus, and fight injustice and evil ideologies that are misleading many who are searching for the truth every day. We must fight the cancer of poverty and ignorance that is causing multitudes to die every day. We must fight mediocrity and establish the kingdom of God here on earth. This is indeed our finest hour.

Recently, I heard a pastor narrate a very interesting dream in which he was visited by two long-dead preachers. These preachers had come back to earth to see how the world was, and how the churches they had founded were faring. They left him at his house to go check things out. After they had come back, he asked them, amongst many other things, what they had noticed, and what advice they had for him. They answered, "This is your best chance to serve God; you must give it your all." They said no one in their churches could even recognize them anymore as founders. The songs that they sang whilst on earth were now considered ridiculous.

Every person in history who made a veritable mark in their day had a sense of urgency about achieving their goals, and realized that it was their time.

Esther is a good example of someone stepping into their moment and making history for eternity. We see the destruction of the Jews imminent by the plot of a palace official called Haman. Esther, who had become queen, was summoned by her uncle, Mordecai, to plead the cause of the Jews before the king. She started to give excuses, like most people do, as to why she could not intercede for the Jews. She explained the fact that she could not get into the presence of the king without being called, which most likely would result in her death. Mordecai, her mentor and uncle, said to her:

"If you keep quiet at a time like this, deliverance and relief for the Jews will arise from some other place, but you and your relatives will die. Who knows if perhaps you were made queen for just such a time as this" (Esther 4:14 NIV)?

Do you realize that you were born for a time like this? You are no accident. It is no coincidence that you were born now in this age. You are not a coincidence, but a God incident. You are not a mistake or a happenstance. It does not matter how you came on the scene of this world. It does not matter if you were born out of wedlock. Remember, there are no illegitimate children, only illegitimate parents. It does not matter if you were born as a result of rape; you can still fulfil your God-given potential. I know of a great American evangelist who preaches the gospel of Jesus Christ and is doing great things all over the world who is a product of rape. If the means of his entry into the world could not limit his divine calling and purpose, neither should you be limited. You and I have in us what it takes to bring salvation to many. You and I have what it takes to feed many children that would die in the next 24 hours without food. You and I have what it takes to reverse impending danger over a city or a nation. This is indeed our finest hour.

Wherefore seeing we also are compassed about with so great a cloud of witnesses, let us lay aside every weight, and the sin which doth so easily beset us, and let us run with patience the race that is set before us (Hebrews 12:1-2 KJV).

I want us to consider some points highlighted in the passage above.

1. The Word of God describes life as a race. We all start running that race from the day we are born till the day we die. It is both a personal and a collective race. It is like a relay; after we finish, we hand the baton to the next person. The Bible says that many of the patriarchs did not receive the promises.

   These all died in faith, not having received the promises... (Hebrews 11:13).

2. We have a cloud of witnesses. What are they doing? The main reason for any person being in the grandstand is to cheer those who are playing. They are cheering us through the Word of God. They're shouting, "Do not give up! Do not give in! Learn from our mistakes; do not repeat the mistakes we made, and keep fighting the good fight of faith! We are all behind you! Persevere! Look up to Jesus for strength!"
   At this stage of the race, it no longer depends on them, it depends on us. We must run. We must win.

3. To run this race effectively, we must get rid of distractions. The Bible calls them weight, excess baggage, things that are not of priority. Can you imagine someone running a race with an Armani suit on, a tie, and holding a suitcase full of clothes? You would certainly consider the person unreasonable. Yet when we allow unnecessary things in our lives, they can become a weight that stops us from running. Mike Murdock says many people fail because of broken focus. Weight sometimes might not be sin, but distractions can stop us from making progress in the main thing we have been called to do.
   Eating heavily late at night can be a weight because instead of resting, the body must work to metabolize food overnight, thus making it difficult to get up early in the morning to spend time with God.

4. It also talks about laying aside sins. Sin is the transgression of the laws of God. Sin is devastating. Sin can sabotage the life's work of a person. Everyone has a weakness, but we must fight to have pure hearts, repent of secret sins, and fight sins of the flesh. Sin will slow a person down, and in many cases, take the person out of the race earlier than planned, for the wages of sin is still death. Sin tolerated is death tolerated. Sin is the undoing of so many gifted and potentially great people. We will do well to get rid of sin in our lives. The reason many continue to enjoy sin is because the consequences do not always kick in immediately (Revelation 2:21-22). God is such a patient God, and gives everyone a fair chance to repent. However, it does not annul the fact that sin is deadly and deceptive. Let me illustrate it by this story.

A young man was walking through the forest once when he came across a small boa constrictor and decided to catch it and take it home. A boa constrictor is not a venomous snake; however, depending on the stage of maturity, it has the strength to wrap itself around its prey and strangle it before swallowing it up. So the young man started to feed the young serpent at home. As time went on, the man had an idea of becoming very famous through the serpent. On special days, such as market days, he would take the serpent to the market square and let it wrap itself around him. The duel was on, and the serpent would pull and the man would push until after a while the man would push off the serpent. The crowd would get rambunctious as they cheered the young man, who thought he was strong. As time went on, the serpent grew in size and strength, whilst that of the young man remained the same. It became more difficult for the young man to push the serpent away. Then came the day when the crowd had attained its largest number and the serpent had almost attained its largest size, and the battle was set. After a while, the young man began to lose strength; eventually his bones were broken, and finally he died. There was a time he could have taken a stick and killed the serpent in less than a minute, but he didn't. That is exactly how sin works. It is very deceptive, and gains strength over time and becomes more difficult to get rid of as a person tolerates it too long—a serpent in Genesis becomes a dragon in Revelation. This is how many have died of addictions. What seemed harmless at the beginning became the very thing that killed them. So we do well to get rid of every weight and sin immediately.

5. We must run the race with discipline and principles. No one wins unless he runs lawfully. Anyone who tries to run the race cheating, stealing or bypassing the rules will be disqualified by God, before whom everything lays naked. There are no shortcuts to winning the race.

A Sense of Destiny

One of my greatest heroes in this generation is Peter J. Daniels, the Australian Christian businessman and philanthropist. For many years, he tried to decipher what made people great. He finally found the answer: *a sense of destiny*. Below are some examples of people who had a sense of destiny:

- Jesus, whose face was set towards Jerusalem
- Paul the apostle, who had a heavenly vision
- Martin Luther King Jr., who had a dream
- John the Baptist, who was the "voice" in the wilderness
- Abraham, who had a promise and was told by God his name would be made great

Many years before he became the prime minister of Britain, Winston Churchill was a soldier who fought in different countries. In a letter addressed to his mum from the battlefront, he wrote that he'd been ambushed by a couple of soldiers, but, miraculously, he faced them with boldness and shot them all. He said at that moment, he realized that he had been preserved for greater things. The rest is now history.

Taking a look at my own life, I can recount a few incidents that almost cost me my life, but, supernaturally, I was saved. I remember vividly when I was between the ages of 4 and 5 years old in a small town called Tobin, in Cameroon. As kids, it was not unusual for us to sneak out of the house to play with the neighbor's kids. At the time, our house was located not far away from one of the main highways. It was on one of such days that I strayed too close to the road, and as I attempted to run away from it, I slipped and fell. At that moment, a Land Rover driving at approximately 80 km per hour missed driving over my head by an inch or two. Needless to say, it scared the living daylights out of me. I dared not tell my parents about the incident, as they might be tempted to kill me themselves for multiple counts of breaking set rules and regulations. I forgot about that incident, but later on in life it would come back to me time and again.

About 10 years ago when I was a student in Germany, I was riding my bicycle one rainy evening. The roads were slippery, and I didn't see a car coming as I crossed the road. When I did see it, I panicked and tried to brake, but, thank God, the elderly couple in the vehicle applied their brakes in the nick of time and my life was saved. It immediately occurred to me that something supernatural had happened. I, too, can echo Winston Churchill, that I was preserved for greater things.

You, my friend, can probably resonate with these experiences, and you may have a catalogue of stories. I dare say you, too, have been preserved for greater things. We must have a sense of destiny and move closer to it. You still have a lot to contribute, even if you are in the twilight years of your life. **You can glean** invaluable wisdom from your past experiences, which could be crystallized in a book to help the next generation. You might be able to train leaders who will not only preserve your legacy, but use it to transform the next generation.

As a mother, you might have the privilege of raising kids who will change the next generation. You might never be in the media or tabloids, but you have a great part to play. Yes, you must have a sense of destiny.

Take, for example, the legendary Mary. Her destiny was to give birth to Jesus. What a privilege to be the mother of the Savior of the whole world! You must constantly live with the reality and the sense that you were created to do something significant, and contribute something invaluable to mankind. In a sense, you are indispensable. You must arm yourself with the knowledge that you are important, and you matter in the grand scheme of things. You must be determined that, before you breathe your last breath, you would

leave behind indelible positive footprints in the sand of time. Like John the Baptist, you are a "voice" of whatever God has called you to be.

I wonder what would have happened if our wonderful, merciful and loving Jesus had not died for the sins of the whole world.

I wonder what would have happened if Winston Churchill had not motivated the powers that be, to summon their strength and resources to fight against Hitler and Nazism.

I wonder what would have happened to the American colony if General George Washington had not fought ferociously to win the American War of Independence.

I wonder what would have happened if Abraham Lincoln had not fought against the inhumane practice of slavery in the United States and made sure that the evil practice was abolished in what culminated in the **Emancipation Proclamation.**

I wonder what would have happened if Martin Luther King Jr. had not fought against segregation and racial discrimination in the USA.

I wonder what would have happened if the legendary Nelson Mandela, together with other noble South Africans, had not endured all the horrendous treatment meted out to them and persevered through those sobering years in prison.

I wonder what would happen if you and I do not rise up to the occasion and bring lasting solutions to the challenges that threaten human civilization.

I pray that as we move with a sense of destiny to fulfil that which we have been called to do, generations in the future will look back at this generation and the things we accomplished for the glory of God and say "this was their finest hour."

AND TO YOU I SAY, THIS GENERATION HAS NOT SEEN THE BEST OF YOU YET!

2

POTENTIAL

Myles Monroe often says that the wealthiest place in the entire universe is not the oil fields of Russia, with all its rich natural resources, nor the gold mines in South Africa, nor different mines all over the world laden with a multiplicity of precious metal and a wide spectrum of useful gases. The wealthiest place in the world is the cemetery, because therein lies a plethora of untapped resources. Trapped within its depths are songs that were never composed, books that were never written, inventions that never came to reality, and businesses that never got started.

To fully grasp the concept of potential, we must first and foremost explore the nature and origin of man.

Humans are the most precious, sophisticated, and complex beings that God ever made, and rightfully so. Man is the crown of God's creation. In six days God created everything, just before He rested, He made the masterpiece of His creation— someone just like him, wow! He made man to manage all that He had created.

And God said, Let us make man in our image, after our likeness: and let them have dominion over the fish of the sea, and over the fowl of the air, and over the cattle, and over all the earth, and over every creeping thing that creepeth upon the earth (Genesis 1:26 KJV).

One of the reasons man is so powerful is because man is made in the very image of the Almighty, Omnipotent, Omnipresent, Omniscient, Everlasting God, the Creator of the universe.

What does it mean to be made in the image and the likeness of another being or person? If you stand before the mirror, you will see your own image. It is not you, but a reflection of who you are.

God made man to reflect who He is. This means man is to have God's values; man is supposed to think the way God thinks and function the way God functions. But also, God created man in His likeness so man could relate and fellowship with Him and understand Him like no other being could. No angel or celestial being is made in the image and likeness of God; just you and me.

And the LORD God formed man of the dust of the ground, and breathed into his nostrils the breath of life; and man became a living soul (Genesis 2:7 KJV).

The word *Human* is a very interesting word. The first part is **Hu,** which comes from *humus,* which is dirt. The second part is **man,** which stands for the spirit-being that God created in His image and likeness. In effect, a human is a spirit enveloped or wrapped in dirt, or earth. So the dirt part allows the human to function in this world, and the spirit allows the human to relate with God and with spiritual things. For God is a Spirit.

God is a Spirit: and they that worship him must worship him in spirit and in truth (John 4:24 KJV).

Every human being is a spirit. The only reason we can relate with God in a special and intimate way is because we are spirit beings. Not only that, but He also made us in His image and likeness, reflecting who He is. Again, no other creature was created in the image and likeness of God; neither angels nor other spirit beings. If you want to know how God is, look at yourself. Remember, your image is not you, but it reflects who you are.

The human mind can seldom fathom the enormity of this. That is why many people operate below what they were meant to be, and probably die without ever realizing their innate potential, never mind attaining it to its fullness. It is a tragedy that many people will die this year without ever discovering the purpose and potential that God has put within them. Meanwhile, some discover their potential, but would allow fear, discouragement, and popular opinion to prevent them from developing their potential and fulfilling their divine destiny.

POTENTIAL DEFINED

Merriam-Webster online dictionary defines potential as existing in possibility: capable of development into actuality.

When someone says you have potential, in essence they are saying that you possess the capacity, qualities, and abilities to become, do or have something in the future. Your potential is what you can become, even if you never become it. Your potential is what you are not yet, but could become. Your potential is what you are and no one knows yet. Your potential is what you could have, but do not have yet. Your potential is what you can do and have not done yet. Potential is that which is hidden and lies dormant, unused and un-manifested. The whole concept of potential relates to the future. It relates to what could be, but is not yet. Therefore, once something has been done, achieved or accomplished, it is no longer potential.

I believe every business has the potential to become better and more profitable. It might take redesigning some processes, repackaging some products, breaking into new markets, etc. Every student has the potential to become better. Every parent could become better at parenting. Every husband and wife has the potential to become a better spouse. In effect, we get married to potential, not perfection. Far too many men have been disappointed, especially at the beginning of their marriage, because they expected their wives on the first day of marriage to rise to the status of a Proverbs 31 woman. Far too many women have been disappointed because they expected a man that would treat them like Jesus; full of love. But they were confronted with a man full of insecurities from past hurts and laden with extra baggage.

God is the author of potential, and since God is limitless, potential is limitless. The word *potential* can be substituted with the word *seed*. A seed has limitless potential. No one in the entire universe could ever predict the potential in a seed. Why? The potential in a seed is limitless. Everyone could possibly count the seeds in a papaya, but no one can count the papaya in one seed. Yet many people have allowed society, people, and popular opinion to predict and to limit what they can become and do.

Back in Cameroon where I was born, my grandmothers understood the concept of a seed. They would rather a person ate a full chicken than eat an egg. They would consider a person eating an egg to be a thief. The reason was that, whilst the person saw an egg, they saw a poultry.

Since the God of potential is limitless, an individual can receive new potential. God is continuously endowing new potential in the form of gifts and abilities and anointings to be used for His glory. You see, it is never too late when God is in the picture.

Potential transcends time. Many people are long dead, yet they are still increasing and expanding their influence through books they wrote, people they trained, institutions they founded, songs they composed, and statements they made. We will discuss more on this in the section on legacy.

God is the embodiment of potential. When God sent His Son Jesus Christ into the world, He was sending potential. He saw the countless believers all over the world that would come to have a relationship with Him and impact the world positively for His glory by believing in Jesus. Today, over 2,000 years later, many people are still being saved and washed in the blood of Jesus. The Bible describes Jesus as the first amongst many brothers and sisters. The seed that is producing many others as people believe on him as their Savior.

For those God foreknew he also predestined to be conformed to the image of his Son, that he might be the firstborn among many brothers and sisters (Romans 8:29 NIV).

In the creation story, God created just one of each animal as male and female, because God put in them potential to multiply. God gave seed-bearing plants to man for food, so the seed could produce over and over again (Genesis 1:29).

God made just one man. As already seen, man is the plural form for the spirit-being God created after His image and His likeness. In the one man was found all men, including "male men" and "female men."

So God created <u>man</u> in his own image, in the image of God created he him; <u>male and female created he them</u> (Genesis 1:27).

When it was time for a female to show up, God did not bother making another man, but simply went where the potential was and pulled out the female, or woman.

...and He took one of his ribs....And the rib, which the LORD God has taken from man, made he a woman and brought her to the man (Genesis 3:21, 22 KJV).

A woman can be defined as a **man** with a **womb**, since the womb of the female is the main part that differentiates the male and female. The womb is the part that receives and incubates the seed. However, the biblical definition of a woman means "that which is taken out of man."

And Adam said, this is now bone of my bones, and flesh of my flesh: she shall be called Woman, <u>because she was taken out of Man</u> (Genesis 2:23 KJV).

One day, God took Abraham and showed him the stars. He was told that as innumerable as the stars were, so shall his descendants be.

He took him outside and said, "Look up at the sky and count the stars—if indeed you can count them." Then he said to him, "So shall your offspring be" (Genesis 15:15).

In essence, God was telling Abraham, "Abe, you have so much potential in you that there is no unit of measurement to quantify it." It is interesting to note that Abraham was over 75 years old when God appeared to him and gave him that promise. Age is no deterrent to an individual's potential when God is involved.

Moreover, Abraham's wife, Sarah, was barren. But you see, God's potential is not limited to circumstances. When God is involved, limitations become a setup for a lifting up.

It is a tragedy in life that most people never discover their potential. I have heard some people say that they do not have any potential. There is nothing more laughable than that. You are loaded with potential, ready to be developed and manifested.

You have something special in you. It is meant to bless the world. Please do not bury it, but use it to glorify God by serving Him and humanity.

Like Benjamin Franklin said, "What is serving God? 'Tis doing good to man."

PURPOSE

To develop our potential, we must know our purpose.

Generally, lots of words are used interchangeably with the word *purpose*. Some of these words include calling, dream, aspirations, vision, and goal.

Merriam-Webster online dictionary defines purpose as the reason why something is done or used. The aim or the intention of something, the feeling of being determined to do or achieve something, the aim or goal of a person, what a person is trying to do or become.

I define the purpose of a person as the reason for being, the *raison d'etre,* and the very *sine qua non* for one's existence. It answers the question of why we came on the scene, what makes our existence necessary at this particular time and place in this prodigious and ongoing human story and in the grand plan of God.

You were created for a purpose. It is your responsibility to find out that purpose for which you were created. The great reward of finding your divine purpose and fulfilling it is primarily yours, and the consequences of not finding it out are also yours.

There are four fundamental questions which most people intuitively ask themselves at one point or the other, which are:

- Where did I come from? A question of origins.
- What is wrong and right? A question of morality.
- Why am I here? A question of purpose.
- What happens to me after I die? A question of destiny.

All these questions should be asked personally, and not generally. For the purpose of this chapter, I want to highlight the question of purpose.

What is your purpose? Everything we see has a purpose. Eyes see, nostrils breathe and smell, legs give balance and are used for movement. Everyone alive has a purpose, whether they know it or not. Everything in the ecosystem has a purpose. Even eliminating a bacteria from the soil will cause an imbalance in the ecosystem. For example, soil contains nitrogen-fixing bacteria that converts atmospheric nitrogen into soil nitrogen that is very important for plant growth. When I was a child growing up in Cameroon, I saw soil being burnt all the time prior to farming. The belief was that burning would render the soil more fertile. All the bacteria useful for the crops were *burnt alive.*

When the purpose of something is not known, there is a high probability of it being abused. The word *abuse* is a combination of two words; *abnormal* and *use.* So whenever something is not being used for the purpose for which it was made, that thing is being **used abnormally,** or simply put, is being **abused**.

A couple of years ago, I lived in the United Kingdom. There was a period when knife abuse became popular. Rival gangs, consisting of mostly teenagers, stabbed and killed each other, especially in the cities of London and Birmingham. It was bizarre and heartbreaking to watch, sometimes on a weekly basis, news of another teenager being stabbed to death.

When those knives were being manufactured, the manufacturer's purpose was not geared for stabbing, but for cutting, chopping or slicing things such as beef, fruits, and vegetables. Using the knife for anything other than its original purpose is plain abuse. In our world today, there is a lot of abuse going on. Abuse of power, wife abuse, husband abuse, time abuse, pastor abuse, child abuse, etc. However, the worst abuse is the abuse of one's life. If you do not discover your purpose in life, you are sure to abuse your life. A person could climb a certain career ladder, business ladder, vocational ladder, and get all the accolades that pertain to that ladder, only to discover at the end of their life that they had climbed the wrong ladder. What agony that can be!

GENERAL PURPOSE OF MAN

And God said, Let us make man in our image, after our likeness: and let them have dominion over the fish of the sea, and over the fowl of the air, and over the cattle, and over all the earth, and over every creeping thing that creepeth upon the earth (Genesis 1:26).

The purpose of a product is in the mind of the manufacturer. The manufacturer establishes the purpose of the product before he sets out to manufacture it. Henry Ford did not manufacture a vehicle and then attempted to figure out what it could be used for. He defined the purpose of a vehicle, then manufactured it. In much the same manner, God had in mind the purpose of man before he created man. Therefore, only God can reveal the purpose of man to man.

The key to understanding the whole purpose of man is hidden in these words "...and let them have dominion." When God created man, he gave man dominion, or "rulership" of the world.

Man was to have dominion over all that was created. However, God never intended for man to have dominion over his fellow man.

What is man, that thou art mindful of him? And the son of man, that thou visitest him? For thou hast made him a little lower than the angels, and hast crowned him with glory and honour. ***Thou madest him to have dominion over the works*** *of thy hands; thou hast put all things under his feet: All sheep and oxen, yea, and the beasts of the field; The fowl of the air, and the fish of the sea, and whatsoever passeth through the paths of the seas. O LORD our Lord, how excellent is thy name in all the earth (Psalm 8:4-9 KJV)!*

God did not leave man to accomplish that by himself, but gave him the blessing to do so. To be blessed means to be empowered to prosper. May you be empowered to prosper in Jesus' name. May God bless you abundantly and may your life take a turn for the miraculous and for significance for God's glory.

And God ***blessed them***, *and God said unto them, Be fruitful, and multiply, and replenish the earth, and subdue it: and have dominion over the fish of the sea, and over the fowl of the air, and over every living thing that moveth upon the earth (Genesis 1:28 KJV).*

It can be seen that God created man to be like him and do what he does. In heaven, God rules supreme. But he gave the earth for man to rule, and trusted that man would do it in a great way. Man is made in His image, and has the very substance of God, to rule the way God rules.

The highest heavens belong to the LORD, but he gave the earth to human beings (Psalm 115:16 ISV).

It was God's intention that man cooperate with Him and have fellowship with Him, and rule the earth. However, through the sin of man in the Garden of Eden, fellowship was broken between God and man (Genesis 3) and the lease of the earth was transferred to Satan (Luke 4:6) who became the god of this world (2 Corinthians 4:4). The purpose of man was thwarted, and man was ostracized from the presence of God.

It is evident that man, through his sin, is the cause of everything that has gone wrong and is going wrong in the world, and not God (Romans 3:23).

JESUS IS THE KEY TO THE RESTORATION OF MAN'S PURPOSE

The ultimate purpose of Jesus coming to the earth was to restore man to his place of dominion on the earth. When man has dominion on the earth by God's standards, the kingdom of God then is manifested on the earth. The kingdom of God is the mind of God, the thoughts of God, the rule of God. The kingdom of God is God's system, or God's way of doing things.

The kingdom of God is, *"as it is in heaven." ...thy Kingdom come, thy will be done on earth <u>as it is in heaven</u> (Matthew 6:10).*

John the Baptist came preaching the kingdom, asking people to repent and enter this wonderful kingdom. Jesus came preaching the good news of the kingdom of God (Mathew 4:17).

However, for the kingdom of God to be established on the earth, God had to first deal with sin, the main reason for man losing this dominion in the first place. The reason is because God cannot bypass the vessel, or the conduit through which He wants to establish His kingdom.

At the cross of Calvary, Jesus died to deal with the issue of the sin in man. Therefore, no believer of Jesus Christ should get stuck at the cross, the place of dealing with sin. Instead we should graduate from the place of *Jesus as Savior* to the place of *Jesus as Lord*.

The kingdom of God is the Lordship of Jesus executed and sanctioned through the believer.

No one is really worried about a person being saved from sin, but when people start to fulfil their purpose by taking their place in the kingdom of God, then the real fight and opposition starts.

From the days of John the Baptist until now the kingdom of heaven suffers violence, and violent men take it by force (Matthew 11:12).

So God's original purpose for man is to have dominion over the earth. God says that His counsel shall stand and He shall accomplish all His purposes (Isaiah 46:10). Therefore, it behooves man to repent of his sins by believing in Jesus, and taking his place in the kingdom of God so God's purposes can be fulfilled through him.

SPECIFIC PURPOSE OF MAN

I knew you before you were formed within your mother's womb; before you were born I sanctified you and appointed you as my spokesman to the world (Jeremiah 1:5 NLT).

"The only thing worse than death is living and not knowing why." Myles Munroe

God has a specific purpose for your life. This is the overriding goal for your life. It is the one thing that defines you and into which you have to pour your life. As we saw in the passage above, God had a specific purpose in the life of Jeremiah; to be a spokesman for God to the nations. You, too, have a specific call and purpose upon your life. You could be involved in other things, but the specific purpose, or assignment for your life is the one thing that determines and guides your decision-making process. Decisions like where to live, whom to marry, what kind of jobs to take, etc.

We have to bring our whole being and energy to bear in the accomplishment of that thing that is the specific purpose of our life. There are many renowned personalities both in the Bible and in the secular world whose life can be defined by one thing. They are involved in other things, but one thing seems to define them. I am not necessarily saying they are all fulfilling the purpose for their lives, for ultimately that is between each individual and God.

When the name Donald Trump is mentioned, people immediately think of real estate. Warren Buffet is associated with investment.

Bill Gates is associated with the personal computer. In the Christian arena, when the name Benny Hinn is mentioned, almost everyone thinks of healing. Mike Murdock is associated with wisdom and prosperity. Billy Graham is associated with evangelism. These individuals are involved in many different things, but there is one thing that stands out and defines them.

God has a specific purpose for your life. It is your responsibility to discover what that specific purpose, or calling is.

But how do we discover this calling, or purpose? I would use the Apostle Paul as an example to make some helpful suggestions.

1. The first step is to get connected to God by believing in Jesus Christ. As we have seen, only the manufacturer knows the purpose of his product. Likewise, only God knows the purpose for which He created you.

   To connect with God means to believe in the Lord Jesus Christ (1 Timothy 2:5, John 14:6). If you are reading this book and you have not yet committed your life to Jesus, I invite you to make that decision right now, and ask Jesus to come into your life. There is no magic formula. All God requires is for you to believe in your heart that Jesus came to earth to die for your sins, then ask Jesus to come into your heart and be Savior and Lord of your life.

   If you declare with your mouth, "Jesus is Lord," and believe in your heart that God raised him from the dead, you will be saved. For it is with your heart that you believe and are justified, and it is with your mouth that you profess your faith and are saved (Romans 10:9-10 NIV).

   Saul of Tarsus, who later became the Apostle Paul, was a Jew who was antagonistic to everything that represented Jesus Christ. He persecuted those who believed in Jesus, and even supervised the death of Stephen. He did all this in ignorance because he considered access to God to be through the Jewish religion.

Though formerly I was a blasphemer, persecutor, and insolent opponent. But I received mercy because I had acted ignorantly in unbelief (1 Timothy 1:13).

But one day, as he travelled to Damascus with letters to persecute the followers of Jesus Christ, he had a life-altering experience with Jesus. The first question he asked was, "...who are you, Lord?" Jesus answered "...I am Jesus Christ whom you persecute." Read Acts 9 in the Bible for the full story of Paul's conversion. The moment Paul realised that Jesus was Savior and Lord, he believed on Him.

It will be really worthless from the eternal point of view to gain notoriety, fame, wealth, prominence and all the good things of this life, and finally perish in hell because the eternal destiny of your soul was not taken into consideration.

For whosoever will save his life shall lose it; but whosoever shall lose his life for my sake and the gospel's, the same shall save it. For what shall it profit a man, if he shall gain the whole world, and lose his own soul (Mark 8:36-37 KJV)?

It is worthless to achieve great feats in life and finally be eternally separated from God.

2. The second step is to ask God to show you His purpose for your life.

Your purpose is not your making, but your discovery. "Lord, what will you have me do?" (Acts 9:6 KJV).

The prayer of dedication is what needs to be prayed. The prayer of dedication is saying to God, "Not my will, but your will be done in my life." The prayer of dedication is being at a place where your will is totally neutral and you open up to whatever God says. Some people go to God to ask for His direction when they already have in mind what they want.

It is not the responsibility of another person to find out what God wants you to do with your life. It is *your* responsibility. Even if someone prophecies it or suggests it, you must know yourself. Your life is not to be determined solely by prophecies of people, but by the Holy Spirit's guidance. The Bible says that as many as are led by the Spirit of God, they are the sons of God (Romans 8:14).

God has many different ways by which He might choose to reveal His purpose for your life; through the Word of God, through people, through a deep conviction, through prophecies and dreams, etc. But ultimately, you should have peace about it within yourself. So, like Paul, pray to God: "Lord, show me what you want me to do with my life." Yes, it is important to seek God, and God will reveal it. God sees our hearts. If we are really serious about His purpose being revealed in our lives, He would surely reveal it to us. It might take seasons of prayer, fasting and protracted periods of waiting before God.

I love those who love me; And those who diligently seek me will find me (Proverbs 8:17 KJV).

I pray that you would be diligent in finding the purpose of God for your life, for no man can truly be satisfied, except when he is at the center of God's purpose for his life. Therefore, make it your number one priority in life to find God's purpose for your life and fulfil it, no matter how long it takes and what it costs. The rewards of fulfilling your divine calling are eternal. At the end, you will be glad you paid the full price to fulfil your divine calling and purpose.

3. Reading the Word of God.

The Word of God is the will of God. The Word of God is the manufacturer's manual. By simply reading and studying the Word of God, you will gradually know the will and purpose of God for your life. The Word of God will direct you into His perfect will for your life, and you will know the purpose for which you were created.

Thy word is a lamp unto my feet, and a light unto my path (Psalm 119:105 KJV).

There have been many times in my life when I was confused, but as I read the Word of God, I got specific guidance as to what I needed to do with my life at that particular stage.

4. Start serving God and serving people. As you seek God's purpose for your life and walk in your present knowledge, be a servant wherever you are. Do what you can do to meet the needs of people. Sitting down with arms folded will not do it. Wherever you are, roll up your sleeves and get to work. As you do that, God will begin to guide you into your purpose. Only a moving ship can be guided, not a stagnant one.

PURPOSE AND PROGRESSIVE REVELATION

Sometimes we might not understand our purpose completely, but as we walk by faith, we will eventually come to understand.

Through faith we understand that the worlds were framed... (Hebrews 11:3 KJV).

Sometimes the purpose of the dream is discovered many years after you have the dream. Initially, it appeared as though the interpretation of Joseph's dream was for him to rule over his parents and his siblings. But the real purpose of the dream was to save lives from impending death through famine. I have heard many people say that they finally understood the purpose of their dreams after many years of pursuing their dreams.

Bishop Tudor Bismarck, the choice servant of God from Zimbabwe, said not too long ago that he just discovered his purpose after over thirty years of preaching. He belongs to the council of African apostles that meet annually to confer on issues affecting Africa. They strategize on how to alleviate ignorance and all its consequent woes such as poverty, hunger, child mortality and a host of other issues pertinent to that continent. My pastor, Mel Mullen, says he now has a better understanding of his purpose after over 40 years of preaching and pastoring, which is to train and equip leaders all over the world to be world changers. No one should be alarmed or disappointed if they do not seem to have a full understanding of their purpose. Start walking in the light you have and God will progressively reveal your purpose as you walk by faith.

Facts about your purpose:

1. Your purpose is unique to you. Each individual is different, with different fingerprints. No leaf is the same as another. God created and designed each one of us differently to fulfil a unique purpose. Even when we do the same thing, there is uniqueness about how we do it.

2. Your purpose is not your design, but your discovery. God is the author of your purpose. Jesus said "...not my will but yours be done."

3. Your purpose is time related. There is a set time within which a person ought to fulfil their purpose. When that timeframe is over, it might never be what it was meant to be. *For everything there is a season, a time for every activity under heaven (Ecclesiastes 1:3)* and furthermore *"He **has made everything beautiful** in its time..." (Ecclesiastes 3:11 KJV).*

4. Your purpose never changes, even though plans and methods in achieving it might change. *For God's gifts and calling never change (Romans 11:22 ISV).*

5. Your purpose has different seasons. Seasons of preparation, anonymity, and of manifestation, etc. The purpose of John the Baptist was to prepare the way for the Lord. He was the forerunner for Jesus. However, he lived in the wilderness until the time that he appeared in public (Luke 1:8). Wilderness connotes a time of obscurity and grooming through difficult challenges. So never be discouraged if you are in a wilderness season. The time of your "appearing" or greatness is coming.

6. God might reveal your purpose directly to you, as in the case of Moses and Jeremiah. At other times, he might reveal it through some other person, as in the case of Paul through Ananias.

7. Your purpose is tied to the purpose of others. Martin Luther King Jr. said that humanity is tied in a single garment of destiny; what affects one directly might affect another indirectly. God said to Joshua: *"Moses my servant is dead; now therefore arise, go over this Jordan, <u>thou, and all this people,</u> unto the land which I do give to them, even to the children of Israel" (Joshua 1:2).*

Seven Reasons why you need to discover your purpose and fulfil your potential

1. Your greatest goal in life is to know your purpose and fulfil it. It is not the responsibility of any person but you.

2. When you find your purpose and potential, you cannot be stopped. So when you die, you die empty, having emptied yourself of all that God put in you. Your gifts and potential are not needed in the grave, but on earth. Elijah passed a

double portion of the anointing upon his life to Elisha, who served him. Elisha, on the other hand, did not pass the anointing on to his servant Gehazi, due to Gehazi's covetousness. The anointing was still in his bones. One day as a man was being buried, raiders arrived and in a hurry the dead man was thrown into Elisha's tomb. When the dead man hit Elisha's bones, he came back to life. You are a solution to a problem on earth. You are necessary. Your gift and your potential are to help you fulfil your purpose and solve a problem.

3. It motivates others to fulfil their potential. There are a lot of things which people think are impossible. When you start fulfilling your potential, they would take off the limitations and begin to fulfil theirs. Pastor Matthew Ashimolowo of Kingsway International Christian Centre was told it was not possible to build a mega church building in London. There wasn't enough land in England was the reason. Well, he started by building a 4,000-seat auditorium. Many are motivated to dream big and fulfil their potential. Many ministers of the gospel have now built mega churches since then. Abraham Lincoln was derided because of his looks and was told he was ugly and could not be the president— well, he did, and still inspires many today to achieve their dreams, including me.

4. You will have to give an account one day before God.
So then every one of us shall give account of himself to God (Romans 14:12 KJV).

5. If you do not discover your purpose and fulfil your potential, that which is yours might be taken and given to another. I read about Kenneth E. Hagin Sr., whom God instructed to write a book. He obeyed, and when he had published the book, a pastor came and told him God had asked him to write that same book many times and he did not. When we do not do what God wants us to do, God will take it and give it to another. Time and tides wait for no one.

6. You will leave the world better than you left it as you contribute to make it a better place. What contribution would you leave behind after you are gone? What would future generations be inspired by because you came on the scene?

7. When you stand before God, you would hear Him say those precious words *"... Well done, thou good and faithful servant... enter thou into the joy of thy lord" (Matthew 25:23).*

DREAMS AND VISION

There are wide and varied definitions of dreams, vision, purpose, goals, aspirations, etc. Sometimes all these words are used interchangeably, and I totally concur that they cannot be separated. However, for the purposes of this subject, I will try to distinguish between them a little bit.

Purpose and potential answer the question of why. On the other hand, dreams answer the question of what. Generally speaking, when you ask a person what their dream is, they will tell you what they want to do or achieve. Meanwhile, purpose answers the question of why they want to achieve what they want to achieve. Purpose will fuel passion to achieve a goal or vision.

More facts about dreams and visions and purpose

1. Sometimes, people carry out a vision for many years before they ever understand the purpose. This is not strange, because we understand from Hebrews 10:38 that the just shall live by faith. Joseph had a dream of ruling over his brothers and parents. But the real purpose was to go ahead

of his parents to save them and the world from impending famine.

2. Just like purpose, your dreams and visions are never about you; it is all about God's plans. So, we'd better get serious and diligent about doing what God has called us to do. The brothers of Joseph thought it was about Joseph, but it had nothing to do with Joseph; it was about God's plan of saving multitudes.

    But as for you, ye thought evil against me; but God meant it unto good, to bring to pass, as it is this day, to save much people alive (Genesis 50:20 KJV).

    Peter had a vision to eat that which was unclean, and he refused. God told him not to call unclean that which God has made clean. The vision was not about Peter, but about what God wanted to do in the lives of the non-Jewish people: the gentiles (Acts 10:15).

3. Hidden in the dream and vision is the purpose.

4. When a person is walking in the vision of God for their life, everything works out for good.

    And we know that all things work together for good to them that love God, to them who are the called according to his purpose (Romans 8:28). Even the things that look bad and horrendous. All the jealousy and the hatred. "...b*ut as for you, ye thought evil against me; but God meant it unto good, to bring to pass, as it is this day, to save much people alive (Genesis 50:20 KJV).*

5. Purpose deals with understanding why you are doing what you are doing, which would be God's original intent. Vision and dream deal with knowing what should be done, and doing it.

6. Dreams and visions need seasons of preparation. It took Jesus 30 years to prepare for his vision. It took Moses 40 years to get ready for the task of taking the children out of Egypt.

7. Sometimes God will have to take you out of your environment and from that which is familiar to you in order to get you ready to fulfil your purpose. Abraham was called to leave his kinfolk. Moses was taken out of Egypt for 40 years. Joseph was taken away from his brothers and sister for over 13 years. I believe a lot of people cannot become what they should be by staying in the country of their birth.

8. Be careful who you share your dreams with. Sometimes the people you love most will be the ones that most misunderstand your dreams. Sometimes close friends will despise your dreams because of familiarity or jealousy. The brothers of Jesus took him for granted, and people in his neighbourhood asked, "Is this not the carpenter's son?" In the case of Joseph, His brothers wanted to kill Him. Someone said, "Do not share your dreams with your half-brothers."

To empower your potential, you must have a dream and a vision. I want you to imagine potential to be like a gallon of fuel, say, gasoline. Gasoline has great potential for use for combustion in a car engine and a host of other energy conversion processes. But unless the gasoline is put to use in an automobile or in other appliances to convert the potential energy to mechanical energy, kinetic energy, heat energy, or other forms of energy, it is utterly useless.

In much the same way, every human being on earth has great potential and purpose for their lives. But without a vision or a dream, those potentials will stay dormant and useless, because there is nothing to cause the potential to come alive and be developed and know fulfilment. Whilst it is obvious that many of these potentials may never be discovered and put to use, it does not nullify the fact that the potential is there.

Over a century ago, there were no aircraft. Many did not even consider that something of that nature was necessary. After all, there were ships, horses, camels and other conventional means of transportation at the time. Was there any potential or purpose for a plane to be invented? You bet! As long as no one saw the need or had that vision, nothing was invented. But alas, many people started experimenting with the possibility of faster transport through aircraft that culminated in the Wright brothers in 1902 designing an aircraft model that could fly people. What a milestone in transportation! We can all attest to the fact that the invention of aircraft for transportation has made life considerably easier, and made travelling much faster.

Everything starts with a dream and a vision. What is your dream? Do you have a vision for your life, or are you accepting everything that life dishes out to you? What are you reaching out to achieve? Are you just waiting and hoping that one day you will win the lottery? Even those who play the lottery with the hope of winning some substantial amount of money spend a considerable amount of money over the years in the purchase of tickets.

There are many kinds of dreams; divine dreams, personal dreams, social dreams, financial dreams, educational dreams, etc. We should all have dreams for the different areas of our lives.

What dreams did you have that are now in the past? What dreams did God put in your heart and you have allowed circumstances to stop you from achieving them?

Whatever dreams you have, they can surely live again. In the 37th chapter of the book of Ezekiel in the Bible, a very interesting scenario developed. The prophet Ezekiel found himself in the valley full of dry bones and God asked him "...can these bones live again?" It is a question that every one of us needs to ask in relationship to our dreams and visions that seem dead. Like many people would answer, Ezekiel said, "Lord, I do not know; only you know." Through the instructions of God and the obedience of the prophet, the dried bones eventually took on flesh and became a sea of humanity.

Your dreams and visions may look dried up and hopeless. But there is a prophetic word in your mouth to speak to your dead, dried, and hopeless-looking vision. "Hear you, vision, the Word of the sovereign Lord; you shall live again."

A couple of years ago in Germany, I got to a place in life where my dreams appeared to be dead. I felt it was over for me. Bless God I have come to know that no condition is permanent. Shortly before leaving Cameroon for Germany to further my education at the age of 19, I had the intention of being a medical doctor. Whilst in Cameroon, I met someone who worked in the oil and gas (petroleum) industry, and was making of lot of money. He advised me to do petroleum so I could make a lot of money like him. After a year of learning and passing the German language exam that qualifies a non-German speaker to study at a German university, I failed to secure admission at any university to study petroleum engineering. I opted for something close—mineralogy. My goal was to spend one year studying mineralogy, and then reapply for petroleum engineering. My one year of studying mineralogy was my most horrendous year as a student. I had no interest in the subject matter, which involved studying the morphology and formation of minerals such as diamonds, gold, etc. Midway through the year, I realized I had made a grave mistake of listening to the wrong advice.

I eventually applied for biotechnology and had a place. I was at the end of my studies, but had three engineering courses that I struggled to pass for one reason or another. These courses were like demonic strongholds. The regulation of the university stipulated that during the course of studies, a student was allowed to repeat only two courses for a third time, which they must pass. Failure to pass at the third attempt would result in being ex-matriculated from doing that program. In my case, I failed two of these courses for the third time each. So, even though I had already done my bachelor thesis and had very good grades, I was ex-matriculated from that biotechnology program on account of failing those courses. I was not allowed to study anything related to biotechnology in the whole of Germany.

I found myself feeling a sense of hopelessness. It looked as though my world had imploded. But in the midst of what seemed to be a gripping yoke of despondency, I looked up to the hills from where my help comes, and I began to encourage myself in the Lord. During that time I wrote a couple poems to help encourage me that were published on www.poetry.com. Below is one of the poems I wrote.

Let Those Dreams Live

Where are those dreams
That flew like streams
Out of your innermost being
So everyone could see?

The sparkle in your eyes
That electrified and spiced
Then great trials came?
Alas, those dreams faded away.

Oh, your speech changed
And boldness waxed and waned
Confidence dampened
Yeah, your passion slackened.
Guess what? The time has come again
For those dreams to be born again.
No circumstance can hinder you
Nor any system obstruct you.

Eventually, I relocated to the UK and did a degree in microbiology. Fortunately, I was able to transfer a lot of credits from Germany, so it took me two years to complete the degree. Eventually I went on to do an MBA in Finance in London. Surely, your dreams can live again. Surely, like the prophet Ezekiel, you can prophecy to dead dreams and visions to come alive.

AND TO YOU I SAY, THIS GENERATION HAS NOT SEEN THE BEST OF YOU!

3

POTENTIAL 2

In this chapter, we will take a look at potential as it relates to some vital aspects of life.

POTENTIAL AND TIME

To everything there is a season, and a time to every purpose under the heaven (Ecclesiastes 3:1 KJV).

God makes all things beautiful in its time. Someone said, "Timing is everything." Sometimes it is possible to get ahead of time and suffer great consequences. The Holy Roman Emperor Joseph II was a man full of good intentions, but he was known for "taking the second step before the first," trying to implement policies too fast, which engendered a lot of opposition and difficulties. On the other hand, there are things that are supposed to be done and are either left too late, or never done at all.

He hath made everything beautiful in his time: also he hath set the world in their heart, so that no man can find out the work that God maketh from the beginning to the end (Ecclesiastes 3:11).

There are a lot of things that can only be done within a certain window of time. These include disciplines like sports. Any potential that primarily requires a lot of physical energy has to be done before and during a certain timeframe or age.

I remember being a fairly talented soccer player. But I never made it to any professional level of play. Now, at the age of 36, when I watch a football game, I have a lot of ideas of what should be done for effective play. But if I were put on the field, I would not be able to play like I should, because I no longer possess the physical strength of a 20-year-old. The most talented athletes probably never make it to the world stage to showcase their talents. These are talents that could bless the world, or even take care of them or their family financially.

Mike Tyson could probably write a bestseller on boxing, but he would not be able to fight with the strength and agility he possessed back in the '80s. Michael Jordan likewise can coach in basketball, but would not be able to play with the ingenuity he possessed when he was much younger. My point is that there are potentials that can be maximized only within a particular timeframe. What has to be done needs to be done now, or it might never be done.

If you are gifted in a sports discipline where a lot of energy is needed, then to attain maximum potential, you have to start early in order to peak at the right time and then exit that arena. In developed countries, kids start attending soccer academies at the age of seven or younger, where they are taught professional football. At that young age, their potential is discovered and honed early. They are taught how to be professionals on and off the pitch at an early age. In developing countries, things are a bit different. Lack of resources prevent a lot of kids from having the chance to go to such academies, if they even exist to start with.

Also, the mentality of those in most developing countries discourages the development of talents at a young age. Sometimes, when a young child is discovered with unusual talent, the parents will do everything to dissuade the child from following that path. Someone told me that his brother was a very good guitar player as a teenager. But he was dissuaded from doing so, and almost got dismissed from school for playing his instrument all the time.

One of the principal reasons is that there is a lot of emphasis put on classroom education. Therefore, parents perceive spending time to develop talents as a form of distraction. A lot of children are advised to focus more on their studies, so that if things do not work in developing their talents, they can have their degrees and certificates to fall back on. This generally leads to a situation where the child has to choose between the two. The way out in many developed countries is that efficient systems have been put in place that make it possible for kids to develop their talent *and* study, while sometimes playing professional sports and earning a lot of money.

Parents should encourage their kids to develop those talents that are tied to physical energy, and get them all the professional help they need.

POTENTIAL AND DEATH

The year was 1990, and the date was September 13. My sister, Lydia, and I were in boarding school. It was the re-opening day of the new school year after a 3-month-long summer break.

It was quite a unique time in my family. For the first time in years, every member of the family was together. My mum had eight kids of her own. I am the seventh child. When I was age two, my parents went and took my cousin, Delphine, from her parents to come and live with us. She became like a twin sister to me, and lived with us till adulthood. So present in the house was my dad, mum and nine kids. The age difference between my eldest sibling and me is 14 years. By the time I got to the age of awareness, my older siblings were no longer living at home. They were in boarding schools in different parts of the country. Whenever my elder sisters came back home from holidays, I thought they were my aunties. Later in life I came to understand their relationship to me.

But this time was special. One of my elder sisters, who had lived in the UK at the time, had come back to Cameroon. For the first time in almost four years, the entire family was together. There was supposed to be some traditional family ceremony coming up sometime after September 13. My parents were sandwiched between taking my sister and me to school, or letting us attend the ceremony and go back to school a few days late. But after some contemplation, it was decided that they would take us to school. Mum and Dad drove us to school, but because we were running late for the customary re-opening day roll call, they dropped us off with our luggage and left in a hurry.

The next day, September 14, was the first day of classes. Sometime before noon, the vice principal of the school came to my classroom to inform me that my sister and I were needed at home. My elder brother had come with my brother-in-law to pick us up with my dad's car. The natural thought was that my parents had decided that it was necessary for us to be part of the family ceremony. You can imagine the ecstasy of going back home, full of anticipation of the goodies that awaited us; goodies that are part and parcel of such a ceremony. I even promised some schoolmates that on my return, I would bring them some goodies.

As we approached our house, I noticed that many cars were parked in front of our house. When we alighted from the car in front of the house, the hands of my sister and I were held, as though to steady us. I noticed the picture of my mum hung up at the top of the garage, but it never rang a bell in my mind. We were both directed through a jam-packed living room as I overheard some women saying, "This is the one she brought to church a few days ago," referring to me.

When we got into the guest room, I saw my mum's lifeless body on the bed, with cotton balls stuffed in her nostrils. At the age of 12, no one really bothered to explain anything to me, so I drew my own conclusions that mum was dead. My sister and I were later led by the hand once again into my parents' bedroom, were my dad laid in the bed, looking 10 years older than the man I had seen just the previous day.

I was told that after my mum and dad had returned home, mum cooked her *last supper* for the entire family. She was not feeling quite well, and had some meeting with some friends across the road, a few minutes' walk away from the house. She decided to go and meet with them for a couple of minutes. When she came back home, she said she had a headache, and decided to lay in bed. She asked for ice blocks to put on her head. Then she called my elder sisters and my dad to her beside. She instructed my sisters to take good care of my dad. Whilst everyone was trying to interpret what she was saying, she started to sing: "I'm going, I'm going, I'm going, I'm going, I'm going to Jesus, take my hands and direct me, I'm going to Jesus," and then breathed her last. Within two hours of complaining of a headache, she was gone.

So it came to pass that on that fateful day, without any premonitions, my mum exited this world. I later learned that she died of an aneurysm, a rupturing of blood vessels in the brain that causes internal bleeding. Unknown to me, she had been a high blood pressure patient for a while. Being a nurse by profession, she was taking the necessary measures to control it. Needless to say, her death was devastating to the entire family, especially owing to its suddenness, and also because it was the first experience for us kids to lose someone so close and dear to us.

No single event in my life has affected me as profoundly as the death of my mum. I began to contemplate my own existence, and life after death. It was at that moment that I realized that life is not what I had thought it was. It occurred to me that everyone on this earth is simply passing through. I realized that everyone living is on a death sentence, even though no one knows the specific time, date and place. It dawned on me that death was something that could be delayed, but never denied. Yes, if you are reading this book, you and I will most likely not be alive in the next 100 years, should the return of Jesus tarry.

Within a year of mum's passing, three other members of our family passed away. What a blow it was to our family. It was these series of deaths that caused me to start thinking deeply of my own eternal destiny, which eventually culminated in me accepting Jesus as my Lord and Savior. Sometimes, it is events like these that cause people to take a more serious look at the meaning of life.

I am greatly empowered by the thought of death because it reminds me of the brevity of life, and of the critical importance to move with a sense of urgency and do those things I ought to do now.

I must work the works of him that sent me, while it is day: the night cometh, when no man can work (John 9:4 KJV).

When the famed motivational speaker Les Brown was once diagnosed with cancer, he said, "I aspire to inspire until I expire." Death can truly inspire us to do what we must do now.

Talking about death in the right way does not mean it will speed up one's death. I remember the first time someone talked to me about getting life insurance. I was not happy about it, because I felt that talking about it would beckon death to come faster. That cannot be further from the truth.

Most people are afraid of death, or even scared to talk about their own death. Maybe they are afraid because they are not sure where they will go when they die. I was always afraid of death until the day I invited Jesus into my life. All fear of death has since left me, and I can join the Apostle Paul in saying: *"O death, where is thy sting? O grave, where is thy victory? For to me, to live is Christ and to die is gain" (1 Corinthians 1:15, Philippians 1:21).*

Our life on earth is measured by time. Death comes to stop our time on earth. The moment death comes, a person has no time again to go to school, to say sorry to the people he has hurt, to play golf, to go on vacation, or to accomplish the well-formulated plans for his life. After death, we will all have to give an account to God on how we lived our lives, and how we used all the wonderful gifts and abilities he endowed us with.

It is appointed once for man to die and after that comes the judgement (Hebrew 9:27 KJV).

So then, each of us will give an account of ourselves to God (Romans 14:12 NIV).

If you are casual with your life, you can easily become a casualty. When it comes to making decisions that have eternal consequences, be cognizant that ultimately, when the time of judgment comes, your pals, wife, husband or children, etc., will not be with you. Be certain that you will be alone.

I will never forget an incident that took place when I was a student at Presbyterian Secondary School Mankon, a boarding school in Cameroon. This incident gave me an understanding of the fact that we ultimately face judgment as individuals. The principal of the school, Mr. Ndzenyuy Francis, was a man of wise sayings. One of his pieces of advice to us students was to understand that we came to school alone, and we would go back to our respective homes alone. So, if we got caught up with the wrong crowd and got dismissed from the school, we would have to face our parents alone. All the students came from different backgrounds. Imagine someone whose parents had to sacrifice comfort and sell properties, such as land, in order to afford the high tuition fees, only for the child to take that opportunity for granted. Children from more wealthy backgrounds could easily play around and not be as accountable, as their parents had all the connections money could buy.

It so happened that a fellow classmate was dismissed for breaking multiple school rules and regulations. Because we lived in dormitories during the school term, it was the custom of the school to take the dismissed student back to the parents in the school van, to make sure they actually got home. In this particular case, the student in question was living behind the boys' dormitory, and his parents' home was up the hill. Standing at the proper vantage point in school, one could actually see everything that was transpiring in front of his parents' home.

So when the school van left with this classmate of ours, it was very devastating to us. I personally was very depressed to see one of our fellow students being taken away from us. A couple of us waited in front of the boys' dormitory and watched the school van emerge a few minutes after leaving the school as it climbed the hill that led to his parents' house and came to a halt. We all watched with a sense of despair as his stuff was packed out of the van in front of his parents' home. It was at that moment that it dawned on me that he had to give an account to his parents for all the money they had spent on him, for all the sacrifices they had made for him. Furthermore, he had to do it without us. Surely we came alone, and we will all leave this world alone. Yes, you will have to give an account of your life alone.

Life on earth is so short. On tombstones, the years of our lives, however long the years may be, are represented by a dash. For instance, 1900–2000. What a dash, and what a short dash. I have never seen a 1-meter, or a two-meter-long dash, but a very short dash.

It is no wonder that Job cried, saying: *"Mortals, born of woman, are of few days and full of trouble. They spring up like flowers and wither away; like fleeting shadows, they do not endure" (Job 14:1-2 NIV).*

Furthermore, the psalmist said, *"Our days may come to seventy years, or eighty, if our strength endures; yet the best of them are but trouble and sorrow, for they quickly pass, and we fly away" (Psalm 90:10 NIV).*

Humanity is mortality. From the first cry as a baby, man has an inevitable rendezvous with death, common to all, inescapable by the masses, unstoppable by the classes, un-deciphered by the best scientist. Death is surely an appointment every man must keep should the rapture tarry. Your cute children and grandchildren must keep this appointment, too. Yes, death is that common denominator that brings every human being to par with each other. And of course, many people live to 100 years with wonderful vitality and strength. However, compared to eternity, that is less than a dot.

Surely, the issue therefore is not death, but how we must live our lives in this short period of time in preparation to meet our God.

It is because of this brevity of life that David said to God: *"So teach us to number our days that we may apply our hearts unto wisdom" (Psalm 90:12 KJV).*

The fact still remains that every living person is on the way to the grave.

Do not live life as though you would be alive in your present state forever. Let us be motivated all the time by the truth that we have just a short time to do what we have to do, then leave the scene.

We have a short time to make an impact, touch humanity, change lives, and ultimately establish the kingdom of God on earth; leaving it a better place than we found it.

Of recent I was at the funeral of a young man who had died in his early twenties. I was reminded of the wisdom in attending funerals.

It is better to go to a house of mourning than to go to a house of feasting, Because that is the end of every man, And the living takes it to heart. Sorrow is better than laughter, For when a face is sad a heart may be happy. The mind of the wise is in the house of mourning, While the mind of fools is in the house of pleasure (Ecclesiastes 7:2-4 NASB).

The late Archbishop Benson Idahosa of Nigeria told his wife and some women in his church before his death to say: "It is my turn," i.e., it is their turn to take the lead in God's work. At the time, they had no clue he was about to exit this earth.

Below are examples of some people who talked about their death.

- Jesus talked about His death often to prepare his disciples for what was coming (Mark 9:38).
- Paul the apostle talked of his death many times. He told a group of people on the beach that they would never see his face on earth again (Acts 20:25).
- The Apostle Peter said *"For our Lord Jesus Christ has shown me that I must soon leave this earthly life"* (2 Peter 1:14 NLT).

Caution: please do not talk about your death to people

unnecessarily. Like I mentioned above, death is one of the worst enemies of man. So when talking about death, it should be done with tact, and with the purpose of inspiring and giving instructions to others about the future. It could be very depressing and unfair to talk about your death frequently, especially to loved ones.

My dad is 82 years old, and his health has not been the best for a while now. Each time I meet him, he tries to remind me that it might be the last time we would ever see each other on this side of eternity. The last time my wife and I paid him a visit, he repeatedly talked about his death to us. The constant mention of death began to create a depressing atmosphere. Finally, I told him that I know he will die and that we are really grateful to God for the long life he has lived, but until that time comes, let's talk about being alive.

Some people talk about their death often to manipulate others and get a pity party going. I know of a man who had a prolonged illness and often said to his wife, "I am going to die." She would be filled with sadness and would beg him to stop saying that, but he persisted. One day when he made that statement, the wife told him that he should go ahead and die and he would be buried. He was shocked and stopped saying that, at least for a while.

However, death can really motivate us to see the big picture of life and of our existence.

- May death motivate you to prepare for eternity (John 3:16).
- May death motivate you to seek God until you find him.
- May death motivate you to love God with all your heart, with all your mind and with all your strength.
- May death motivate you to evangelise and tell people about the love of God through Christ Jesus. How shall they believe without a preacher? (Romans 10:14).
- May death motivate you to get up from bed early to get the job done, strive to continuously develop your capacity, and fulfil your destiny.

- May death motivate you to stop procrastinating and start that business, write that song and book, open that savings and investment account.
- May death motivate you to always try as much as possible to be at peace with all people (Romans 12:18).
- May death motivate you to love that wife, that husband, those kids, and really be appreciative of the blessings and privilege to have them in your life. The greatest regret of most people on their deathbed is that they did not spend enough time with their loved ones.
- May death motivate you to invest in your kids and grandkids, for they are the next generation to carry on your legacy.

The two last things that death should motivate you to put in place as soon as possible are a will, and some life insurance. I want to talk elaborately on these two below.

A WILL

Having a will is being responsible to your family. May death motivate you to write your will and keep your house in order. Most families are torn apart because someone died without writing a will, leaving their family members to grab whatever they think is their inheritance. My dad wrote his will at the age of 30, when he was still a policeman. When he told his friends about it, they all screamed and asked him, "Martin, what are you doing?" The general fear is that if you write your will, it means you will soon die. That cannot be further from the truth.

Writing your will means that you are aware of the fact that you have just a certain timeframe to live, and that there are things you ought to do to keep your house in order should God call you home. My dad is now 82 years old and by the grace of God, has outlived most of his friends.

During my pre-teen years, I would find pieces of paper with names on them in my father's suits and jackets; names of my brothers, cousins and relatives. It took me a while to figure out that those names were written down so that when he died, there would be little confusion as to who owns a specific suit or item.

Writing your will does not mean you will die soon. For the love of your family members, write your will as soon as possible.

LIFE INSURANCE

May death spur you to get a life insurance policy to protect your investments, such as your house. By the way, life insurance is an investment, too. Life insurance is an income replacement that covers all the bills and expenses of a family if a parent or spouse passes away. Many families have been kicked out of their homes when a parent passed away. The wages of one person could no longer meet the payments of the bills. All of a sudden they were left with nothing, because there was no life insurance policy to take care of the family financially. I come from a culture where people generally do not consider life insurance important. Most people believe in blessed assurance. You need both the spiritual and practical, if you can afford it. We need to be responsible to our family by taking out a life insurance policy.

POTENTIAL AND GIFT

You have gifts that are unique to you. Everyone has a gift. No one is without gifts. Whilst it is true that we all differ in gifts, and some people seem to have more gifts than others, it still stands that everyone is gifted in one way or the other. A lot of times, gifted people do not even know they are gifted. Since their gifts come naturally, they sometimes think everyone can do what they can. Most often, it is someone else that discovers the special gifts in people, and not the possessors of the gifts themselves. For example, boxers, soccer players, dancers, and singers exhibiting their gifts in unconventional places have been discovered by others.

Unfortunately, a lot of gifted people have not made it to the world stage for one reason or the other. One of the keys to the financial success and freedom of an individual is discovering their gifts and taking these gifts to the marketplace. Your gifts, refined and developed, will bring value to the marketplace, and people pay for value.

Could it be that you have a great gift and you are letting the gift go undiscovered and unused? It's time to start developing your gifts.

A gift is a natural endowment. Unlike a skill that is learnt, a gift is natural; however, it has to be groomed, or honed. There are gifted singers who just sing naturally. Others have to go to a music school or to a voice trainer to learn how to sing. A gifted singer does not need to learn the art of singing, only how to fine tune their gift. The same can be said of cooking. Some people are naturally gifted cooks; they need no recipe to come up with something delicious. Others have to use cookbooks; if not, the meal with not be edible. Learn how to identify your gifts and use them to empower your potential and fulfil your purpose. This might mean taking the challenge of trying new things and exploring new ventures. You might need to register in a school where you can be properly trained on developing your gifts.

Paul the apostle encouraged Timothy to stir up his gifts (2 Timothy 1:6). This means your gifts can be dormant if you do not use and develop them. It has been said "what you do not use, you will lose." The more you use your gifts, the more you become adept at using them. Do not let your gift die of neglect. At yet another time, Paul reminded Timothy not to neglect the gift in him (1 Timothy 4:14). This means that a person can neglect their gifts. Please, whatever gifts God has given you, do not neglect them. You might have the gift of management and administration, giving, encouragement, sports, etc. Develop your gifts and use them to fulfil your divine purpose and bless humanity.

One of the main reasons why people do not use their gifts is fear.

FEAR

Fear is not just an attitude; it is a spirit that comes to short-circuit people from using their gift.

Therefore I remind you that you <u>stir up the gift of God</u> which is in you by the laying on of my hands. For God has not given us the spirit of fear, but of power, and of love and of a sound mind (2 Timothy 1:6-7 King James 2000 Bible).

Paul was encouraging his spiritual son, Timothy, to stir up the gift that was in him. Paul further continued with the conjunction "for." A conjunction connects a preceding statement with the following one. Paul continued, "For God has not given us the spirit of fear..." Keeping the verses in context, it is easy to see that the main reason Paul identified why Timothy and many people are not stirring up and using their gifts is because of the spirit of fear; fear of what people might say, fear of failure, fear of criticism, etc. Maybe the reason you have not been able to use your gifts in church, at school, or in the marketplace is because of fear.

To overcome this fear, you have to make a decision to confront that fear and take action by using your gifts.

Let us take a look at different ways in which the spirit of fear manifests in people's lives.

Fear of Man

Make a decision that you would not fear people, for the fear of man is a trap (Proverbs 29:25). If you want to use your gift and fulfil your purpose and destiny, you must decide never to fear man or let what people think stop you. We respect leadership and value constructive criticism, but never be afraid of man. The fear of man will take you out of God's plan for your life very fast. If in doubt, ask King Saul in the Bible.

'....I feared the people, and obeyed their voice" (1 Samuel 15:24 KJV).

King Saul was given instructions to annihilate the Amalekites and destroy everything in their land, but because he was afraid of the people, he preserved the best of the sheep for sacrifice. His kingdom was taken and given to another; to David.

Fear of Criticism

We must never be afraid of criticism or what people may say, if we are to do that which God wants us to do. We live in a democratic world in which people are entitled to their opinions. Never take someone's criticism personally. There is constructive criticism which we can learn from, but that is not what I am talking about. Never allow the negative criticism of people to stop you from using your gifts. Someone once said, "If criticism could kill, the skunk would have long been extinct." Whatever people may say about your gift, go ahead and use it anyway. I am incredibly blessed by a poem found in Mother Theresa's home for children in Calcutta. I have included this poem below titled "Do it anyway"

DO IT ANYWAY

People are often unreasonable, irrational, and self-centered. Forgive them anyway.

If you are kind, people may accuse you of selfish, ulterior motives. Be kind anyway.

If you are successful, you will win some unfaithful friends and some genuine enemies. Succeed anyway.

What you spend years creating, others could destroy overnight. Create anyway.

If you find serenity and happiness, some may be jealous. Be happy anyway.

The good you do today, will often be forgotten. Do good anyway.

Give the best you have, and it will never be enough. Give your best anyway.

In the final analysis, it is between you and God. It was never between you and them anyway.

So I say to you, people may criticize you when you use your gifts to fulfil your purpose; use you gifts anyway.

In the end, you have to please the one who has called you, and to whom you have to give an account. You are accountable to the one who gave you the gifts, and that is God, anyway.

Fear of Failure

You have probably heard it said before that "Failure is not final."

Failure is just an experience, and not an end. To succeed in this life and to do what God has called us to do, we must never be afraid of failure. Failure is a learning experience. When a person fails in doing something, that person learns how *not* to do that thing in that particular way again. One of the hallmarks of entrepreneurs is the mastery over the fear of failure, because entrepreneurship is risk taking.

Thomas Edison, who brought the light bulb to a point where it was marketable, is said to have tried and failed over 1,000 times before succeeding.

Never be afraid of failing. Many people have never succeeded in much, because they have never failed. They play it safe and have a false philosophy that they can only do things if success is guaranteed, without realizing that sometimes failure is the very building block of success as a person persists.

FEAR OF REJECTION

He was despised and rejected by mankind, a man of suffering, and familiar with pain. Like one from whom people hide their faces he was despised, and we held him in low esteem (Isaiah 53:3 NIV).

In life, rejection is par for the course. There is probably no great achiever who has not been rejected. Anyone who has never been rejected or known any form of rejection has never attempted accomplishing anything significant. Therefore, rejection should not stop you from applying for jobs, or from pressing on to achieve your dreams. Jesus came to pay the penalty for the sins of the world. You would think he would have been celebrated by those he had come to save, but all he got was rejection. That never stopped him. He kept pressing on till he accomplished his mission. We, too, will know a lot of rejection, but as we press on, we will succeed. Sometimes life will not give you what you ask for, but what you demand. So we should ask, and if we do not get what we desire, we should seek and finally knock, and keep knocking until the door opens (Matthew 7:7).

HOW TO OVERCOME FEAR

- **Seeking the Lord.** *I sought the LORD, and he answered me; he delivered me from all my fears (Psalm 34:4).* Seeking God through the Word of God, through prayers and waiting on the Lord will release the power of God in a situation to dispel all fear.
- **Developing a strong love walk**. The spirit of love will cast away the spirit of fear. *There is no fear in love. But perfect*

love drives out fear, because fear has to do with punishment. The one who fears is not made perfect in love (1 John 4:18 NIV).

- **Getting knowledge**. Most often, people are afraid when they do not have enough information about something they want to get involved in. Do due diligence in getting all the information you need to give you the confidence to move on.

- **Refuse to allow past failures to sabotage future successes**. Sometimes because people attempted something in the past and failed, it discourages them from trying again. Affliction will not rise up a second time (Nahum 1:9).

  May you succeed the second time as you try in Jesus' name.

AND TO YOU I SAY, THIS GENERATION HAS NOT SEEN THE BEST OF YOU YET!

4

MIND-SETS AND BELIEF SYSTEMS

For as he thinks within himself, so he is. He says to you, "Eat and drink!" But his heart is not with you (Proverbs 23:7 NASB).

We are the product of what we think. The way a man thinks is who he is. If anyone needs to change, they need to change first and foremost in the way they think. The sum total of an individual's thoughts is what he is and what he is becoming. Our thoughts impact on our belief systems and convictions. Our destiny is not determined by circumstances, but by what and how we think. Everything is dependent on our perspective; how we see and interpret life. Our achievements on earth can be classified by the way we think and believe.

Someone can give you his money, but to become like him and achieve like him, you have to think and believe like him. Those who are aggressive and urgent about winning souls for Jesus and those who don't, all have a way of thinking that is mutually exclusive and diametrically opposed to each other. The rich and poor have different ways of thinking. Poverty and wealth are all mind-sets and not based on what people possess. That is why, given time, everyone will operate at the level of their mind-set. Research has shown that over 90% of those who win a million dollars in the lottery become bankrupt within three years.

In his book *Mind Monsters*, Kevin Gerard states that our thoughts are trains that take us to a destination.

Where we are now in every sphere of life is a direct function of the way we have been thinking over the years gone by. Some people think that there is no life after death, so they live their lives in a certain way that does not take into account eternity. How shocked they will be when they find out eternity is for real. Hopefully it will not be too late.

Why is it very important to change the way you think? This is because thoughts are the blueprints of every action we take; be it a thought we conceive, or a thought we allow to go unchallenged in our minds through suggestion from the spiritual realm. What we think determines how we feel and react; it determines our attitudes. How we react determines what we do. What we do determines our character, and our character determines our destiny. This is the reason why the Bible instructs every believer to renew their mind and not their spirits (Romans 12:2).

What happens in the mind for a long time will eventually manifest, whether we like it or not. Thoughts find expression in the natural. Myles Munroe rightly said that we should renew our mind and not get rid of it.

If we think something is impossible we will never achieve that thing, because we are convinced that it cannot happen.

Many years ago, before the advent of airplanes, it was inconceivable to many that such an invention of cosmic proportion could come to fruition. But today, a man can have breakfast in Africa, take midday snacks in Europe, have dinner in North America, and spend the night within in Asia the same 24-hour window by the invention of a plane. The Wright brothers, who invented the aircraft, were able to accomplish such a feat because they thought it was possible.

Without taking into account challenges that are a natural part of life, our present condition, situation, and circumstances are a direct function of our thought life.

This means that your prosperity is one thought and decision away. Healing in your marriage is one thought and decision away. Starting to fulfil your potential is one thought and decision away. Having a relationship with Jesus is one thought and decision away.

Someone said, "There is nothing as powerful as a made-up mind." Make up your mind to do all it takes to fulfil your divine purpose, then start by renewing your mind.

Because everything starts with the way we think, it is imperative that we change our mind-set.

It is paramount and a must to change our mind-set if we have to change our destiny and become what God intended for us to become.

Changing your mind-set

Therefore, I urge you, brothers and sisters, in view of God's mercy, to offer your bodies as a living sacrifice, holy and pleasing to God—this is your true and proper worship. Do not conform to the pattern of this world, but be transformed by the renewing of your mind. Then you will be able to test and approve what God's will is—his good, pleasing and perfect will (Romans 12:1 NIV).

The Bible encourages us to constantly change the way we think. Mind-set stems from two words; **mind** and **set**. It means that the mind has been set to think in a particular way. It is just like cement used for construction. When the cement is mixed with water and put into a pillar, it sets and becomes solid after a while. That is why the mind is the most difficult thing to change, and it takes work and diligence to change a mind that has set. A wrong mind-set comes through ideologies, physical environment, thoughts, and belief systems passed down from generation to generation. Let me illustrate how the mind of an individual can set over a period of time when a physical limitation gets into the mind.

A piranha and a goldfish were put in an aquarium. However, the piranha would eat up the goldfish. Each time a new goldfish was put in the aquarium, the piranha ate it unfailingly. To prevent this, a transparent glass divider was installed in the middle of the aquarium in order to separate the two fishes. Each time the predatory fish attempted to come close to the goldfish, it would bump its head against the transparent glass. After a while, the glass divider was removed, but the piranha never ate the goldfish again. Each time it came near the goldfish, it would think of the pain of hitting its head against an invisible barrier.

Another interesting scenario is that of training a certain elephant. The elephant had a chain tied to a leg, and the chain tied to a tree. Each time the elephant attempted to go beyond a certain distance from the tree, the chain on its leg would restrain it from doing so. Eventually the chain was untied from the elephant's leg and from the tree. However, the elephant would not go beyond a certain periphery of the tree. The chain had left its leg, and had now entered into its mind. The brain of the elephant had now been trained not to go beyond a certain point.

We must recognize how these wrong mind-sets have limited us throughout our lives and will continue to limit us unless we change them. We are not only supposed to change our mind-sets, but also become agents of change. If we apply these principles with diligence and focus, we will eventually have victory.

Below are some suggestions on how to change our mind-set.

Reading and meditating on the Word of God.

The first way of renewing the mind, or changing the mind-set, is through the Word of God. The Bible is the will of God to man. It is the revelation of God's thoughts, plans, purpose and intentions for man and for the world. Man is in trouble because he thinks and acts contrary to the Word of God.

The thoughts of God and the ways of God are higher than those of man. Thankfully, we do not need to try and figure out what these high thoughts and ways are. His thoughts and ways are in the Bible, available for us to read and meditate upon.

As the heavens are higher than the earth, so are my ways higher than your ways and my thoughts than your thoughts (Isaiah 55:9 NIV).

The Word of God contains wisdom on how to live right with God and man, from business to relationships, dealing with money, overcoming difficulties, etc.

May grace and peace be multiplied to you in the knowledge of God and of Jesus our Lord. His divine power has granted to us all things that <u>pertain to life and godliness,</u> through the knowledge of him who called us to his own glory and excellence (2 Peter 1:2-3, ESV).

By meditating on the Word of God on a constant basis, the old mind-set gets replaced with the new mind-set, and the life of God begins to flow in those areas of a person's life where the mind has been renewed.

The unfortunate fact is that a lot of people read the Word of God, but they do not take time to really meditate on the Word of God habitually because they are too busy. If it took so many years to let a certain mind be set, then it will take some time for the new mind to be set as well.

Study this Book of Instruction <u>continually</u>. Meditate on it day and night so you will be sure to obey everything written in it. Only then will you prosper and succeed in all you do (Joshua 1:8 LT).

The King James Version of the Bible renders the same passage as follows:

This book of the law shall not depart out of thy mouth; but thou shalt meditate therein <u>day and night</u>, that thou mayest observe to do according to all that is written therein: for then thou shalt <u>make thy way prosperous</u>, and then thou shalt have <u>good success</u> (Joshua 1:8 KJV).

Lasting prosperity and good success in all areas of your life are tied to the Word of God alone.

But his delight and desire are in the law of the Lord, and on His law (the precepts, the instructions, the teachings of God) he <u>habitually</u> meditates (ponders and studies) by day and by night (Psalm 1:2 AMP).

The following habits will help you change your mind-set:

- Make a habit of reading the Word of God on a daily basis
- Make a habit of studying at least one Scripture a day, and finding out the meaning and application in your life
- Make a habit of writing down new things you learn from the Word
- Make a habit of memorizing Scriptures
- Make a habit of sharing what you have learned with others, to edify them
- Make a habit of practicing the new things you learn from the Word of God

Listening and speaking the Word of God

What we hear and what we confess have a great impact on changing our mind-sets. This is what the communists used to change the minds of people in communist countries. All the radio stations ran the words all day long: "Communism is good, capitalism is bad." People were forced to say it until they started to believe it.

It is important to make a habit of listening to the Word of God all the time and speaking it out. Use the Word of God to challenge every thought that comes to your mind that is contrary to the Word of God.

Casting down imaginations, and every high thing that exalteth itself against the knowledge of God, and bringing into captivity every thought to the obedience of Christ (1 Corinthians 10:5 KJV).

Strongholds are in the mind. These include thoughts, experiences, and philosophies that have been in our minds for a very long time. These strongholds are contrary to the Word of God and our divine destiny. We sometimes defend them and hold onto them because we a convinced they must be right. The Word of God has the power to expose these erroneous thought patterns and to pull them down as we keep studying the word and speaking it with authority.

Reading on a wide variety of subjects by different authors

There are a lot of experts who have written books on different subjects. There is practically a book on every subject. Books on how to raise kids, how to find a spouse, how to train dogs, how to invest, how to create wealth, etc. However, everything should be filtered through the Word of God. This is very important. There is a lot of spooky stuff in print that would get a person into big trouble were they to apply it.

By association

We can change our minds by our interaction with people who will help and challenge us to change our mind-set. We tend to take on the thoughts and mind-sets of those we hang around with all the time. Something about their way of thinking rubs off on us. On the other hand, association with the wrong group can be deadly.

Blessed (happy, fortunate, prosperous, and enviable) is the man who walks and lives not in the counsel of the ungodly [following their advice, their plans and purposes], nor stands [submissive and inactive] in the path where sinners walk, nor sits down [to relax and rest] where the scornful [and the mockers] gather (Psalm 1:2).

Attending seminars and conferences

Pay to attend seminars and conferences that will impact your life positively and help to change your mind-set.

AND TO YOU I SAY, THIS GENERATION HAS NOT SEEN THE BEST OF YOU YET!

5

LEAVING PAST BEHIND

PAST FAILURES

The past can be one of the greatest limitations that prevents a man from moving forward and fulfilling his potential. As we have seen, potential relates to the future, and therefore the past must be left behind. The past is a mountain that we have to scale. Very few people have a past they can really be proud of. Many people look back and see mistakes and errors they've made, and this can greatly impair their ability to move forward and accomplish the things they need to accomplish. That is why "rags to riches" stories greatly inspire us.

These stories help us to understanding that surely, nothing is impossible. In fact, the past is a great deterrent and enemy to empowering our potential.

There are many people who are convinced that they could never become anything worthwhile in life because of their past mistakes, sins, etc.

However, the whole purpose of Jesus' coming was to deal with our past. He starts by forgiving our sins when we ask for forgiveness, and then gives us a fresh start, a hope, and a future.

He has removed our sins as far from us as the east is from the west (Psalm 103:12 LT).

For I know the plans I have for you," declares the Lord, "plans to prosper you and not to harm you, plans to give you hope and a future" (Jeremiah 29:11 NIV).

This truth is reiterated many times in the Bible, both in the Old and New Testament. God is a God of new beginnings.

Forget the former things; do not dwell on the past (Isaiah 48:18. NIV).

He who was seated on the throne said, "I am making everything new!" Then he said, "Write this down, for these words are trustworthy and true" (Revelation 21:5).

What no man or system can do, God can do in a second. We are prone to judge people based on their past. Sometimes we even judge ourselves based on our past experiences. For instance, say you failed at starting a business before. You should not take that failure as an omen and come to the conclusion that business is not for you. The reason for failure might have been wrong timing, or insufficient preparation.

You have probably heard it said that "your past is in the tomb, and your future is in the womb" or that "yesterday is history, tomorrow is a mystery, today is a gift, and that's why they call it the present."

You must go to any lengths to unclutter yourself from the negative effects of your past.

Life is too short to allow the past to stop you from moving forward. We all acknowledge that there are things in the past we need to deal with in order to move forward. We might need to forgive ourselves and forgive others and make certain restitutions. You may need to go back to school in order to cancel any disadvantage of illiteracy. The point I am making is that you can overcome the limitations of the past.

It does not matter what ills or atrocities you might have done in the past; God is able to forgive you and give you a new start. You might be on death row, charged with murder. God will forgive you if you are willing to ask for forgiveness, and he will give you a new start and a meaning for your life

Through determination and the help of God, there is nothing in your past that is trying to hold you back that you cannot overcome.

It is amazing how God has used a lot of people whose past would be considered despicable by many. God does not consult our past to determine our future.

Paul the apostle, the writer of two-thirds of the New Testament, was one such man. He was one who had persecuted the church of Jesus Christ greatly, and even supervised the stoning of Stephen.

In due season, Paul was miraculously converted to Christianity. He found himself confronted by the stark reality of his past each time he wanted to make progress in God. His past tried to take the wind out of his sails and stop him dead in his tracks. The past is a very powerful force that can keep us from moving forward. Paul finally came to the realization that for him to move forward, he had to deal with his past. He therefore made it the goal of his life to forget the things of the past that wanted to hold him back, so he would be able to press towards the wonderful things that laid ahead of him.

No, dear brothers, I am still not all I should be, but I am bringing all my energies to bear on this one thing: Forgetting the past and looking forward to what lies ahead (Philippians 3:13 TLB).

For you to press towards your divine calling, you have to make it a goal in your life to forget the things of the past. Forgetting the past does not mean erasing it from your memory. You will always remember the things that have happened in the past, and the things that you have accomplished. Forgetting the past means that it has no power to prevent you from moving forward. Say, for instance, you are offended or betrayed by someone.

By the way, it is part of life to be offended. However, the problem is holding onto the offence. In this case, forgetting would mean to forgive the person who offended you. Forgetting might mean to stop talking about the issue over and over, because that might peel off old scars that were already in the process of healing. This is a conscious decision, which might need a lot of help from others through counselling and prayers.

Forgetting means when you see a person who hurt you in the past, those old feelings of hurt don't come rushing back. These are the feelings that can hijack future opportunities to move ahead. Those feelings and thoughts have to be dealt with through continuously forgiving the person (Matthew 8:22).

Leaving the past behind might mean moving away from tradition and getting rid of old and destructive habits and appetites. Below are some suggestions on how to stop the past from preventing you in accomplishing your purpose.

1. Identify and confront the things in your past that are holding you back. In fact, write a long list of all these things. Classify them all under three categories.

   a. Sins against God. Ask for forgiveness.

   b. Sins against others. Ask for forgiveness from them.

   c. Things committed against you. Forgive those who offended you.

   I know this sounds simplistic, and I totally agree. Certain things really do need time to overcome, and might take a process. But you must make that decision to let go of the past. What lies ahead of you is more important than what lies behind you. You cannot afford to sabotage your future by holding on to the past. Sometimes you might need to deal with things one at time.

2. Realise that every day is a new start.
   "Today is the day the Lord has made, we will rejoice and be glad in it" (Psalm 118:24).
   What you could not accomplish yesterday, you will be able to accomplish today. God's mercies are new every morning. The reason we always look forward to a new year is because we believe there is fresh grace and an impetus to help us to accomplish what we could not accomplish in the previous year.

3. Recognise that everyone has a past. It may be hidden, or secret, but everyone has a past. It is only by the grace

of God that we can all lift up our heads and square our shoulders. *For **all** have sinned and fallen short of the glory of God (Romans 3:23 KJV).* So do not look at your case as a special case with no way out. God is in the redemption business, and he not only forgives us, but wipes our slates clean.

Those who are making it in life and achieving great things are those who have learned not to allow their past to hold them back. Neither should you let your past hold you back.

PAST SUCCESSES

"The greatest enemy to your progress is your last success." Myles Munroe

Another deterrent to the empowerment of potential are past successes. A lot of people are grounded by past successes. This is the reason why many people become stale and complacent.

In Joshua 1, we see God reminding Joshua of the fact that Moses was dead.

*After the death of Moses the servant of the Lord, the Lord said to Joshua son of Nun, Moses' aide: "**Moses my servant is dead**. Now then, you and all these people, get ready to cross the Jordan River into the land I am about to give to them—to the Israelites (Joshua 1:1-2 NIV).*

Joshua was the closest person to Moses, even closer than Aaron. When Moses died, Joshua was the one anointed to take the children of Israel across the Jordan and into the Promised Land. But he kept looking at the past. He probably thought to himself, *who could possibly do what Moses had done, considering all the stupendous miracles that had been wrought through Moses?* So, God had to come and remind him that Moses was dead. In other words, "Let go of the past!" God was about to begin a new chapter, for God is constantly on the move—from faith to faith and glory to glory.

There is a tribe in Cameroon where the people are called "I was." The people of this tribe have a history of being successful, and then losing everything later in life. If you were to sit with them to have a conversation, all they would talk about are their past glories, "...When I was." Sometimes in churches, people give testimonies of what God did in their lives so many years ago. This is always wonderful, but most often people want to be sure God is still doing those things today.

Life is constantly evolving, and we must be in sync with what God is doing. Dwelling on past successes is one of the reasons businesses become irrelevant and go out of business overnight. It would be ludicrous for someone to still be producing cassette tapes with the expectation of making good sales when we are in the era of the flash drive and the iPod for the storage and playing of music.

No business can succeed in this generation if it depends on past glories. Microsoft co-founder Bill Gates once said that at any given time, Microsoft is two years away from being bankrupt. He cannot depend on the glories of the past to sustain and guarantee the success of the future of Microsoft.

Holding on to past successes is what makes churches that were vibrant in the eighteenth Century become religious and full of tradition today—because they base their methods of worship on what God did over 200 years ago.

We must realize that yesterday's records are today's standards. The record time it took Ben Johnson to run a 100-meter race 25 years ago is now the standard. Hussein Bolt has set a new record which might become a standard tomorrow.

As Myles Munroe aptly captured it, "The worst enemy of your progress is your last success." In other words, the worst enemy of the best is the good we have already achieved.

We must be grateful for past successes, but we should not get stuck there. Holding on to past glories will turn a person into a dinosaur, or make him become as "dead as a dodo."

You must set new standards for yourself. You must beat your own records. You must pray more, and with more knowledge and accuracy. You must pray with more fervency and urgency.

You must study more, love more, and give more. A lot of people turn their past successes into a monument, then build a shrine to worship there. A PhD of 1980 has no value in today's market if the holder has not been improving his knowledge through continuous education.

Abraham Lincoln said, *"I do not think much of a man who is not wiser today than he was yesterday."*

To move into your future, you must learn to put the past in the right perspective. You must make a commitment to constantly improve on the past, rather than to keep glorifying it. You surely cannot move into the future until you let go of the past. To lay hold of what is ahead, you have to let go of what is behind. To enter into the future, you have to come out of the past.

The children of Israel who left Egypt that were 20 years and older could not enter into the Promised Land because they still held on to the past. Caleb and Joshua were the only two exceptions. The others still yearned for the garlics and leeks of Egypt.

As long as you are still overly impressed by your past and what you have accomplished, your past becomes your future. God has no use for a man or a woman who keeps dwelling on their past, no matter how glorious it was. In a sense, you must "hate" your past to desire and move towards your future.

Lot's wife turned into a pillar of salt as she looked back at Sodom and Gomorrah.

Lot's wife is an eternal memorial of what happens to those who gaze too long at the past instead of looking to the future. Stop talking a lot about the past, and start talking about the great future that lays ahead of you.

AND TO YOU I SAY, THIS GENERATION HAS NOT SEEN THE BEST OF YOU YET!

6

POTENTIAL AND LIMITATIONS

There are a lot of factors that stop people from empowering their potential and fulfilling their destiny. We have already dealt with some of these factors in previous chapters. In this chapter, I would like us to have a look at a few more limitations. Even though there are many external limitations, such as the environment a person grows up in, most of the critical limitations are internal limitations, such as attitudes and destructive habits. Through capacity building and faith, we can overcome these impediments. Sometimes a person must deal with these issues on a continual basis until victory comes. There are other things that must go immediately, because what is tolerated, un-confronted, and un-contested will thrive.

1. IGNORANCE

My people are destroyed from lack of knowledge (Hosea 4:6 NIV).

One of the greatest problem in the world is ignorance. The nations of the world that are drenched in unbelievable poverty, disease, infant mortality, disorders, and all the plagues that make life almost unbearable have one thing in common—ignorance. Many people are not fulfilling their potential because of the lack of knowledge. Knowledge truly is power.

In order to fulfil potential, three areas of ignorance have to be tackled.

A. **IGNORANCE OF YOUR IDENTITY**

Every challenge in life is targeted first and foremost at your identity. Who are you? I believe that identity crisis is the biggest of all the problems in the world. Jesus understood this, and established who He was from the very beginning of his earthly ministry with statements such as these:

- **I am** the resurrection and the life (John 11:25)

- **I am** the bread of life (John 6:35, 48)

- **I am** the light of the world (John 8:12, 9:5)

- Before Abraham was, **I am** (John 8:58)

- **I am** the door (John 10:9)

- **I am** the good shepherd (John 10:11)

- **I am** the way, the truth, and the life (John 14:6)

- **I am** the true vine (John 15:1)

Jesus asked His disciples, "Who do men say I am?" and He further asked them, "Who do you say I am" (Mark 8:29-27)?

Jesus' greatest contention with the religious leaders of His day was that of His identity. The primary reason they wanted to kill Him was not because of His background, color, language, height, education, or amount in His bank account; but because of who He was and who He claimed to be.

Jesus answered them, "I showed you many good works from the Father; for which of them are you stoning Me?" The Jews answered Him, "For a good work we do not stone You, but for blasphemy; and <u>because You, being a man, make Yourself out to be God</u>" (John 10:32-32).

When Herod understood that the wise men had come to worship

the King, he felt threatened and sought to kill Jesus. The identity of Jesus as King threatened Herod.

Most people are not aware of who they are. They have bought into a lie told by someone else about them. Myles Munroe says we ought to be suspicious of people's opinions about us. Only God has the right to define who we are because He created us. Never let your circumstance define who you are. Never let a sin you committed define who you are. Never let an incident that took place in your life define who you are.

All warfare in your life is a result of who you are or who you could become. Your success or defeat in life is predicated primarily on your knowledge of who you are, and walking in that identity.

The sons of Sceva who attempted to cast out demons from a man without establishing their identity got the beatings of their lives from the demon-possessed man and all fled away naked. But the demon knew the identity and authority of those it respected. *"Jesus I know, and Paul I know about, but who are you" (Acts 19:15 NIV)?* Your authority over situations in life is tied to knowing your identity.

A prince would live as a pauper all his life if he did not know who he was. Many people in the Bible that were used by God in a mighty way did not see themselves as anything of worth. God had to first of all help them to have the right portrait of who they were before he could use them. Let us look at some examples in the Bible.

Gideon

In Judges 6:11-24, we find the story of the call of Gideon. When the angel met Gideon at the threshing floor of Ophrah, he was called a ***great man of valor.*** He was told who he was before being given the assignment to deliver Israel. But Gideon took the time to explain that he was the least in his father's house, from the weakest tribe of Israel and besides, if God was with Israel, why were they in bondage by the Midianites? It is interesting how we sometimes see ourselves differently from how God sees us. We will never do the things God has called us to do if we do not see ourselves as God sees us.

Jeremiah

Jeremiah is another example of someone called by God to be a *spokesman* to the nations. Jeremiah explained that he was just a child, and God forbade him from looking at himself as a child and commanded him to carry out what he had been called to do (Jeremiah 1).

Moses

Moses was called to bring the children of Israel out of Egypt. He started to look at himself based on his inability to talk. God told Moses that Aaron would be a voice or prophet to speak for him, and Moses would **be a god** to Pharaoh (Exodus 7:1).

The above and others are examples which show that man has always looked down on himself, differently from what God sees him to be.

Therefore if any man be in Christ, he is a new creature: old things are passed away; behold, all things are become new (I Corinthians 5:17 KJV).

The moment a person gives their life to Christ, they immediately take on a new identity. Their citizenship, inheritance, and abilities all change.

We are seated in heavenly places in Christ Jesus. We are a chosen generation, a royal priesthood, a peculiar people, kings and priests for God, above only and not beneath. Our citizenship is in Christ. We are God's masterpiece, created in Christ Jesus unto good works (1 Peter 2:9).

Establish who you are in Christ through the Word of God and know your identity. Your future depends on your identity.

B. IGNORANCE OF WHAT YOU POSSESS

A lot of people are not aware of the gifts and abilities residing in them. A man died in abject poverty. When people came to clear out his stuff from his room, they found a painting which was appraised at a million US dollars. The man was rich for most of his life, but he had no clue. That is the case of well over 90% of the world's population. Many are dying without ever knowing what potential and abilities they have.

Moses felt confounded standing in front of the Red Sea, with Pharaoh and his army chasing from behind. When Moses cried out to God for help and God asked him, "What have you in your hands?" God asked him to stop crying and stretch out the rod over the Red Sea for the waters to part. The Red Sea did a moon walk in two different directions, and the children of Israel passed through on dry ground. Moses had the very rod of God, but he did not know what he had.

The boy with the two fish and five loaves of bread in the Bible thought that was all he had. However, in the sight of God, he had a restaurant chain.

Michael Jordan might have thought all he had was a basketball in his hands, but really he had the ability to turn that into hundreds of millions of dollars.

What do you have? What gifts and abilities do you have? Could it be you have a food franchise in you and you are unaware? Many years ago, comedians made people laugh for free, but not anymore. They found out what they had. The stand-up comedy industry today is a multimillion dollar industry.

C. IGNORANCE OF YOUR ABILITIES

I can do all things through Christ who strengthens me (Philippians

4:13).

Many people are ignorant of what they can do. God gives us the ability to do the things he has called us to do.

I watched the inspiring film of the true life story of Ben Carson, the African American neurosurgeon credited with being the first surgeon to successfully separate conjoined twins joined at the head. As a young man, he was tormented in class and was considered inferior and dumb. But he applied himself to studying, and emerged as one of the greatest surgeons in America. He stood tall above all his classmates in terms of accomplishment.

You might not be good in one thing, but there is definitely something you are good in. If you find and develop that potential, there is no telling how far you could go with it. One of the greatest keys of success in life is finding the area of your calling and potential, and sticking with it.

It is your difference, your unique abilities that are celebrated in the world, and not your similarities with others. It is your difference that brings value to the marketplace.

In the days of trade by barter, people went to the market to trade their goods for something different, which they lacked. Can you imagine everyone taking potatoes to the market on a set market day? Imagine the potato-dumping that would have taken place.

Find out what you can do, spice it up with your uniqueness, take it to the marketplace and see what can become of it. McDonald's and Burger King all sell burgers and fries, but they taste different. Surely you can do all the things God has called you to do as he strengthens you.

2. EVIL COMPANIONS

Be not deceived: evil communications corrupt good manners (1 Corinthians 15:33 KJV).

Evil companionship is another great hindrance to potential. The adage "Birds of the same feather flock together" bears some truth. The companions and friends a person keeps will determine what they become.

Companionship talks of your circle of close friends. Those you hang around with are influencing you more than you might be aware. If you hang around with someone for long, something about them will rub off on you. You will start talking and thinking like them. Jesus' disciples began to act like Him after a while (Acts 4:13).

I remember asking one guy in church whom I heard using the F-word very liberally, why he did that. He said to me, "When a person spends a very long time in the toilet (washroom), that person tends to stink." He meant that he had been hanging around the wrong crowd.

Get rid of toxic relationships. Stay with relationships that inspire you, and bring out the best in you. Hang around people who will help you fulfil your potential.

Many have been destroyed because of keeping company with the wrong people. Many have died before their time because they associated with the wrong people. One such person was Amnon, the eldest son of David, who was obsessed with his half-sister Tamar (Absalom's sister). It was not until Amnon's friend Jonadab advised him on how to sleep with Tamar that Amnon's destruction was sealed. Years later, Absalom plotted the murder of Amnon as revenge for raping his sister (2 Samuel 13).

He that walketh with wise men shall be wise: but a companion of fools shall be destroyed (Proverbs 13:20 KJV).

Each time God wants to bless a person, he introduces someone into their life. Each time Satan wants to destroy a person, he also introduces a person into their life.

Blessed is the man that does not keep company with evil doers.

Oh, the joys of those who <u>do not</u> follow the advice of the wicked, or <u>stand around</u> with sinners, or <u>join in</u> with mockers (Psalm 1:1 NLT).

Jesus had to get rid of all the naysayers. When he was about to raise the dead, some were laughing and making a mockery of Him. He took only those who believed with Him. What I am becoming today is because of those I hang around all the time. Abraham Lincoln said, "You will be in five years as you are now except for the friends you keep and the books you read." If you hang around people for long, you could start living out their consciousness and conclusions.

If you live around negative and cynical people all the time, you will become negative and cynical.

As I take inventory of my past decisions, I realize how they have been affected by the counsel of those I hang out with. Jesus had many levels of relationship, which were clearly defined. Jesus had seven main levels of relationships, and each level had different levels of interaction and influence in His life. The relationships were with:

- God the Father and the Holy Spirit.
- The three disciples: Peter, James and John.
- The twelve disciples.
- The seventy disciples.
- Israel.
- The church.
- The world.

Therefore, it is very important to carefully define every relationship. Make sure that those you are very close to are helping you become a better person, and inspiring you to achieve your goals as you inspire others as well.

A story is told of an eagle's egg that was mixed with those of a chicken to be incubated by the mother hen. In the fullness of time, the mother hen hatched all the eggs. The eagle started off living like chickens. It never attempted to fly to great heights. But one day, the eagle spread its wings and a draft of air lifted it up and it started to fly. The eagle did not go back to have a farewell party before leaving the chickens. It left and never came back.

To fly to the great heights of your potential, you will have to sever some relationships promptly. I have never in my life eaten eagle BBQ, but I have eaten chicken countless times—why? Because the destiny of every chicken is the human stomach. To avoid being eaten up by life, poverty, destruction, etc., you will have to say no to some relationships.

3. DISCOURAGEMENT

We must learn the skill of fighting discouragement. One of the deadliest enemies in your life is discouragement. We have to recognize that the world in which we live is a fallen world. Sometimes, Murphy's Law seems to want to take precedence in our daily lives. Murphy's Law states that "whatever can go wrong will go wrong." Therefore, we have to learn to stir ourselves to ride against the tides of negative things that try to bring discouragement. Like King David, we have to learn to encourage ourselves in the Lord. Negative things might happen *to* us, but we should not allow those things to happen *in* us.

Guard your heart above all else, for it determines the course of your life (Proverbs 4:23 NLT).

We must learn to work by faith and not by sight *(2 Corinthians 5:7).* We must look past circumstances and believe on the promises of God. With the eyes of faith, we must see the victory that lies ahead of us. For the victory ahead is greater than the present situation.

For everyone who has been born of God overcomes the world. And this is the victory that has overcome the world—our faith (1 John 5:4 NIV).

We must see the possibilities in what might look impossible and grim.

...If thou canst believe, all things are possible to him that believeth (Mark 9:23 KJV).

We have to declare boldly like David, "The Lord is my light and my salvation, whom shall I fear?" We have to be assertive like Paul in declaring, "I can do all things through Christ who strengthens me." And yet at other times all we have to do is to stand still and see the salvation of the Lord. Like Ralph Waldo Emerson said, "Let us be silent, that we may hear the whisper of God."

We all need to draw encouragement and inspiration from the biographies of those who rose from the quicksand of despair and discouragement to the mountaintops of great achievement. If they overcame discouragement, we, too, will overcome.

Finally, we need a strong support system. We all need to encourage one another. Every man sooner or later will have to deal with discouragement, but those who succeed are those who have learned to overcome discouragement.

4. LAZINESS

The hand of the diligent will rule, while the slothful will be put to forced labor (Proverbs 12:24 ESV).

Laziness is a great sin. Being busy is not the opposite of laziness. There are a lot of lazy people that are busy doing nothing in particular, and that in itself is a form of laziness. Laziness is not just wasting time, but is also lack of commitment to find out one's purpose in life and fulfil it. Laziness is lack of commitment to undertake the necessary preparation that would make the process effective and efficient.

Abraham Lincoln once said, "Give me six hours to chop down a tree and I will spend the first four sharpening the axe."

To empower potential, we must fight laziness like a plague.

Laziness sometimes manifests itself in the following ways:

- Lack of diligence. Diligence is quick attention to assigned tasks.
- Laziness also manifests itself through procrastination, the art of always putting off stuff until tomorrow. Procrastination has been said to be a destiny assassin. Many have been destroyed because they did not act promptly. Many people have put off the call of God to repent and to commit their lives to Jesus, and then it was too late.
- Lack of focus, poise and drive.
- Always making excuses. Many people suffer from chronic *excusitis*, the disease of making excuses all the time. Examples of excuses are—it is cold outside, I cannot go to work today; it is too hot; there might be a lion outside on my way to work so I should stay home; the government is letting us down, that is why we are not succeeding; etc.
- A great desire to rest and sleep all the time. One of my professors in business school said he slept for five hours a night as a student. According to him, you have no right to be sleeping when you have not accomplished anything significant.
- Refusal to think. Someone once said, "Some people would rather die than think." Thinking and brainstorming can significantly reduce the time, energy and resources spent on a project.

- Mental, physical and spiritual laziness. For any person to succeed, that person must develop themselves mentally, physically, and spiritually. Some people are very diligent mentally, reading and exercising their intellect, but neglect the spiritual and physical aspects that are very important as well.
- Overly theoretical. Always having ideas with no action taken to accomplish even one task. Do not let your ideas die as an embryo. Do what it takes to birth your ideas by taking action.
- Unfinished projects. Laziness is the undoing of many. The lazy person goes to the forest and kills a deer, but does not cook it up and allows it to spoil.
- Always blaming others for negative outcomes or failure in their lives.
- Lack of vision, goals, and plans for life.

To empower potential and fulfil our destiny, we must avoid laziness by being diligent. Diligence is defined as quick attention to assigned tasks, moving fast and swiftly.

Seest thou a man diligent in his work? He shall stand before kings, he shall not stand before obscure men (Proverbs 22:29 KJV 2000).

He that deals with a slack hand becomes poor, but the hand of the diligent makes rich (Proverbs 10:4).

5. ENVIRONMENT

Another limiting factor to the development of potential is geographic location. Every creature has an environment in which it flourishes. For instance, the natural habitat of fish is water. However, waters differ both in the volume, saltiness, currents and other factors that will determine to what extent a particular fish flourishes and attains its full potential. Experiments have shown that if a shark is put in an aquarium, it never grows past a certain size. But when the same shark is taken out of the aquarium and put in the sea, it grows to its full length.

In much the same way, our environment will determine how far we can go in attaining our potential. By this I mean being in God's timetable for your life relative to geographic location. Living in Europe for over 14 years, I saw many people who were prosperous in Africa and decided to move to Europe in search of greener pastures, and almost became beggars. On the other hand, some who were beggars in Africa moved to Europe and are doing very well. So every individual should be sensitive as to where they should be living in a particular period of their lives.

Abraham was asked by God to leave his people and move to a land that would be shown to him. Lot, Abraham's nephew, was asked to leave Sodom and Gomorrah.

Preacher and bestselling author Cindy Trimm, who was a senator in her home country of Bermuda, obeyed God's leading and moved to the United States, where she has become a spiritual force to be reckoned with. She has an international ministry and travels all over the world preaching the gospel and empowering potential in the lives of many.

For others, moving to America would be suicidal to the call of God for their lives. Each person must ask themselves, "Is this where God wants me to be at this time of my life?" Do not stay at a place when it might be clear to you that your time there is over.

AND TO YOU I SAY, THIS GENERATION HAS NOT SEEN THE BEST OF YOU YET!

7

CREDIBLE MENTORSHIP

Everyone needs a mentor. A mentor is a role model. A mentor is one with experience. A mentor is a teacher. A mentor can be younger or older than you.

A mentor is one who believes in your potential and will help shape you for success. It might be someone in the field in which you are venturing, or a motivator. A mentor is someone who has been where you are going. Mike Murdoch says there are two ways of learning—through pain or experience. Experience is learning through mistakes, whilst mentorship is being guided into truth and the right path.

Those who have mentors and follow their instructions normally have less scars in life. Those without mentors go through life trying to figure out things by themselves.

In the context of a nuclear family, God designed man to be the pillar of his family and a mentor to his wife and children. If we take a closer look at kids from communities with no fathers at home, there is generally a noticeable dichotomy of what these kids become, compared to kids that grow up in homes with a fathers. The fathers who are supposed to be first mentors to these kids are missing in action. The boys normally do not have any reference point of manhood, and might join gangs and are incarcerated in their early teens. The women typically find themselves in abusive relationships because they have not grown in an environment where marriage is modeled, to see firsthand how a man treats a woman. Nevertheless, there are exceptions in every generality.

Mentorship is critical. There are many people willing to guide you and hold your hand and make your journey in life easy. It is your responsibility to find them and do what it takes to get to them. I have come to realize that even though these people are willing, they do not have time to waste on people who are not serious. That means to get a mentor, you have to be serious. You should not desire what they have, but what they know, their mind. To desire what they have makes you a parasite, and not a mentee.

In the Bible many had mentors—Timothy had Paul, Elisha had Elijah, and Ruth had Naomi. One of the greatest people who has been a mentor to me is Dave Willows. He has greatly impacted and imparted so much in my life. When we first met, he had just taken oversight of the church I used to attend, where I was a minister of the gospel. He immediately took interest in me after he listened to me preach. He told me he would like to mentor me, along with others. This was an answer to prayer, as I had been praying for years for a mentor.

He began connecting me with other preachers to help shape my theology and character. He would even give me different subjects from the Bible to study, and to preach a 10-minute message in front of him as though to a crowd. Then he would critique my preaching, my diction, my body language, eye contact, and everything that goes with the art of preaching. At his home, for the first time, I had to do a formal study of the Christian doctrines and study of other preachers like Spurgeon, Wesley, John Calvin, etc. He helped me to pronounce words in the right way, especially because having lived in different countries and speaking different languages, it is not uncommon for me to pronounce a word wrong.

My point is, a mentor can teach you in an hour what would have taken you a decade to figure out. I have been incredibly blessed to have such a mentor in my life, along with many others who have mentored me in different areas of my life over the years.

We need mentors in different areas of our lives. We can have a spiritual mentor; for instance, our pastor—or any person who is spiritually mature—to hold our hands as we go through the challenges of life. It could be a male or a female, older or younger, it does not matter, as long as they are helping us and are being a role model. They must be people we respect and love, because we cannot learn from someone we do not respect.

To get a mentor, look and pray carefully. Once you see someone who fits the bill, mention politely that you would like to be mentored by them. If they accept, ask for expectations and requirements. Remember, *you* need the mentor, and not vice versa.

Sometimes mentorship is not free. Mentorship might mean attending a seminar or a conference. You have to put great value on what you want in life and what you want to achieve. Mentorship sometimes requires travelling to other places, countries and across oceans.

There is also mentorship through books and the Internet. Do not start any venture without mentorship. Invest in books. Develop a reading culture. Read history and biographies.

However, the greatest of all the mentorship manuals is the Bible, and the greatest mentor is the Holy Spirit.

So, the first person you need to ask to be your ultimate mentor is the Holy Spirit. Paul Yonghi Cho has written on how important it is to make the Holy Spirit our senior business partner in all we do.

But the Advocate, the Holy Spirit, whom the Father will send in my name, will teach you all things and will remind you of everything I have said (John 14:26 NIV).

When the Spirit of truth comes, He will guide you into all the truth; He will tell you about the future (John 16:13 NLT).

The Holy Spirit is the one from the future. He knows everything about everything. He is omnipresent, omniscient and omnipotent.

Happy, fortunate, powerful, and to be envied is the man that is intimately acquainted with the Holy Spirit, for that man's life will flourish in all areas as he is taught all truth and taught about the future and how to prepare for it.

However, we need both the Holy Spirit and a human mentor.

AND TO YOU I SAY, THIS GENERATION HAS NOT SEEN THE BEST OF YOU YET!

8

CHARACTER AND YOUR POTENTIAL

"Your gift may bring you before kings and great men, but only your character can keep you there." Anonymous

Character is the foundation on which everything stands. Without this foundation, everything will fall apart. Too often, people have achieved greatness, but the lack of character turned their achievements into rubble. Billionaires have committed suicide, those in the film industry with nine-figure bank accounts have ended their own lives. Every year we hear of celebrities involved in scandals. Sometimes these cause them to lose contracts with major companies with whom they had endorsements. Those who had once been hailed and celebrated now become a ridicule and a laughing stock in the media and on tabloids.

If the foundations be destroyed, what can the righteous do (Psalm 11:3 KJV)?

As you develop your gifts and you become influential and prosperous, you will need to have the strength of character to deal with the responsibilities and perils that come with success, or being in the limelight. This responsibility of success is very great, as people begin to look up to you as a role model. It is important that you set a good example. I am not talking about perfectionism, and trying to live up to the standards and expectations of people. Neither am I talking about being a people pleaser. However, success and leadership not only come at a great price, but also to stay a leader for a long time has a great price tag attached to it. Leaders are held to higher standards. For each new level of success, there is a new devil waiting to take you out. Therefore, you must do all it takes to have the strength of character and be blameless before God and man (Romans 12:17).

You will need to develop a strong foundation of love, because people will be jealous. Loved ones will misunderstand you and criticize you. Many will malign you and concoct all kinds of lies to discredit you. Love will always keep you strong. Love might mean forgiveness, or praying for people. People might even pay investigators to watch your every move. Sometimes what you say might be misconstrued and put in the tabloids or on the Internet. The simple-minded will believe it. It might even affect your sales as a businessman, or affect church membership. Sometimes people will set up men or women to try and seduce them into a sexual scandal. All these and many others are realities that everyone who seeks to achieve their full potential, and be their best for God, and impact the world, must be aware of.

It is critically important that we strive to build impeccable character, to be pure before God, and to stand the pressures that come with success. Someone once said that more people have been destroyed by success than any other thing.

The greatest success is not in what we accomplish or achieve, but rather that we become more like Jesus. Let me deal with just a few areas of character to be developed.

Sexual Purity

We have to develop a thick skin when it comes to sexual immorality—first of all in our thoughts, and then in the way we carry ourselves. Sexual immorality is perhaps one of the greatest crimes of this generation. Some consequences of sexual immorality include:

- Destroyed marriages due to infidelity
- Loss of career
- Death due to Sexually Transmitted Diseases (STDs)
- Ministries coming to ruin because of sexual immorality by a pastor

It is not the physical effects of the sexual sin, but the spiritual effects that can be the most devastating. Even though God's forgiveness is readily available, sometimes people struggle for the rest of their lives with the guilt of what they did.

- I was on the streets evangelizing one time in Mannheim, Germany. I met a man who looked forlorn and dejected, downing a bottle of whisky. I approached him and started telling him of God's love through Jesus towards him. To my utmost surprise, he told me he had been a Christian. He had committed adultery, and when his wife found out, she divorced him. He said he had lost everything. But the saddest part of the story was the guilt he carried. He felt God could never forgive him again. I had to take some time to explain to him that God's love is boundless, and he would forgive anyone who would come to him in true repentance.

- We must totally depend on the grace of God to keep us from immorality, and we must cultivate a holy fear and reverence for God. The Bible warns us to flee fornication or sexual immorality. Flee means to run as in terror. There is a formidable agenda from hell to take out many potentially great people from the race of life through sexual immorality. We must be as wise as a serpent and harmless as a dove. We live in a generation were almost everything is being advertised with sex—from cars to drinking water. Therefore, we should constantly be watchful of our thoughts, and discipline our flesh. We should realize that the sinful desires of the flesh will keep raging against us until we die. Many who have been ignorant about these have found themselves in a pretty terrible mess and wondered why. Through applying ourselves to the Word of God, prayer, avoiding situations where we are prone to fall, and being accountable to trusted people, we can live a pure life starting with purity in our hearts. We should also avoid "all appearances of evil" that can engender a scandal, especially when we start getting to places of success and influence.

- Generally speaking, knowledge of ourselves and any potential weakness in this area should help us to do what is necessary to avoid temptation in the first place. This might mean using computer software to block certain sites on our computer, or asking hotel staff to block pornographic channels when we are on the road on business or ministry. We should be even more watchful when we are tired, feeling lonely, and away from our spouses for those who are married. Some husbands travel everywhere with their wives. Simply put, we must do everything, and pay the price to stay pure at all time.

If your hand or your foot causes you to stumble, cut it off and throw it from you; it is better for you to enter life crippled or lame, than to have two hands or two feet and be cast into the eternal fire. If your eye causes you to stumble, pluck it out and throw it from you. It is better for you to enter life with one eye, than to have two eyes and be cast into the fiery hell (Luke 18:8-9 NIV).

In context with our subject, this passage means that we ought to take every radical step to prevent sexual immorality. It might mean leaving a country, a job, or a city, to save your life. Like Joseph who ran from Potiphar, so we ought to run from sexual immorality.

Integrity

Our word should be our bond. We should be people of our word. Let your yea be yea and your nay be nay (Matthew 5:37). There is a slang in German which means neither yes nor no. The word YES in German is "JA" and NO is "NEIN." So when something is in-between yes and no, people combine the two words into one, "JAEIN." We should mean what we say and say what we mean. We must develop a consciousness of the things we say, and not just say things out of emotion when we really do not mean them.

There are many cultures I know where people are very casual with words, and say things with no intention of following through on their words. As men and women who seek to build God's kingdom, we must seek to be people of the highest integrity. This of course is not to bring us under any form of bondage, where we feel obligated to follow through on an engagement even when circumstances beyond our control prevent us from doing so. In such cases, we should be quick to apologize and explain to the other party why we are not able to keep our word.

We must also learn to say no in a firm but polite manner when we cannot render a favor to someone. Sometimes out of fear of offending people we have found ourselves in a big mess because we have not trained ourselves to say no when we cannot fit something or someone into their schedule. Always trying to please everyone sometimes can be very dangerous on a person's wellbeing, as it can lead to being burned out. It is better not to commit to something than to commit and not do it. To be a person of character, we must learn to say no sometimes.

It is amazing that the main thing that differentiates God from man is telling lies. The reason we can totally trust in the faithfulness of God is because he cannot lie.

God is not a man, that he should lie; neither the son of man, that he should repent: hath he said, and shall he not do it? Or hath he spoken, and shall he not make it good (Numbers 23:19 KJV)?

It did not say that God is not man that he should not eat, cough, sneeze, etc. This implies that the main thing that differentiates man from God is lying. Human beings are generally expert liars. We should therefore get rid of lies in our lives whether it is a *white lie, black lie, pink lie* or *green lie.* **A lie is a lie**. Generally, fear and pride are the two main reasons why people lie. So we must deal with these two issues in our lives.

Finances

One of the greatest areas in which we need to develop character is in dealing with money; firstly in our hearts. We must learn how to deal with money in a way that glorifies God. We must learn to see it for what it is, a tool, and not a god to be worshipped. For the love of money is the root of all evil. We constantly examine our hearts to deal with any tendency to love money. The love of money can be reflected when all decisions are made based solely on money, e.g., accepting a job, even when it jeopardizes our relationship with God, puts our marriage at stake, etc. God wants us to be good stewards of money and good investors of money, but it does not mean we should invest in things that do not glorify him. We live in times when people will do anything for money, and from the proceeds of great abomination give to charity in an attempt to pacify their souls from guilt. The Bible did not say as many as are led by money, they are the sons of God, but rather *"as many as are led by the Spirit of God, they are the sons of God"* *(Romans 8:14).*

Secondly, we should learn to manage our money. Many people have been destroyed not because they stole money, but because they mismanaged money. When a person is ignorant of the rules that govern money, and of the financial laws of the country, they can easily find themselves in a deep pit.

To avoid this, hire financial planners, financial advisers and accountants and other professionals to help you make sure the books are right. Do not walk in ignorance, for ignorance is not bliss—it is destruction. What you do not know may be killing you.

My people are destroyed for lack of knowledge (Hosea 4:6. KJV).

It is not enough to say that God knows your heart and intentions. God might understand, but we are not just dealing with God, but with man. Therefore, we ought to do everything right, both in the sight of God and man.

For we are taking pains to do what is right, not only in the eyes of the Lord but also in the eyes of man (2 Corinthians 8:21 NIV).

Humility

We must avoid pride in all its subtlety. We must never forget the days of small beginnings as we develop ourselves and God promotes us. As we become more successful and influential, we should never forget where we started.

Many people do not empower their potential because they are too proud to learn from another.

On the other hand, many people have been trusted with authority and they could no longer relate with their subordinates. I remember a man who was promoted to a certain position in a school. Before his promotion he was approachable, but as soon as he was promoted, he developed an air around him. He could no longer relate to people without letting them know "I am the boss." A lot of people have become legends in their own minds and worship themselves. The late Archbishop Benson Idahosa of Nigeria said, "Never allow your status to make you a statue."

Pride goeth before destruction, and an haughty spirit before a fall (Proverbs 16:18 KJV).

One of the success secrets of King David was his humility.

For those who exalt themselves will be humbled, and those who humble themselves will be exalted (Luke 14:11 NLT).

When David was being pursued by his son Absalom, he was severely insulted by Shimei, a clansman of King Saul. David restrained his generals from killing Shimei. At other times, he had opportunities to kill King Saul, who sought after his life, yet David was still careful not to strike the Lord's anointed. Whenever I read the story of David, I find tears streaking down my cheeks, touched by the humility and meekness of this great king. Over and over, King David expresses his dependence on God. He acknowledges his fears, his disappointments, his failures, and expresses the fact that God alone is his trust and hope.

Abraham Lincoln once said, "Nearly all men can stand adversity, but if you want to test a man's character, give him power."

Most people start out trusting in God, until they attain great heights. Then they become self-dependent, and seem to ask God to back off. However, it is important to realize that without God we can do nothing. In the natural, children are taught to be less

dependent on their parents as they mature. However, God wants us to be more dependent on him as we get more mature. God is the author of life; he gives us breath, strength, and wisdom. Without God, we would not be able to get up from bed each morning. Every day we get up in the morning is a resurrection, for sleep is a kind of death. Someone sleeping is oblivious of what is going on around him or her, and very vulnerable to a lot of elements. But God protects us as we sleep. Wow, what a great God!

We must always remind ourselves of the fact that it is a privilege to be blessed, successful, and to have influence over people. It is not a right. History is laden with examples of dictators and leaders who thought it was their birthright to rule people with obstinate pride. Most of these dictators ended up being murdered or locked behind bars, or exiled to other countries where they lived the rest of their lives in misery.

- To overcome pride means we have to constantly depend on God and His Word for strength and direction.
- We have to constantly pray for His power. Prayerlessness is one of the greatest hallmarks of pride. Prayerlessness is man depending on himself and not God.
- We have to constantly check our motives for doing things to make sure that it is to serve God and humanity, and not for self-aggrandisement.
- We have to be constantly thankful for all the successes bestowed on our endeavours, for without God, we can do nothing (John 15:5).

Developing Potential and Character

Potential and character are normally developed during periods of adversity, difficulty, challenge, and even in obscurity. Just like a negative is developed in a dark room, sometimes it takes extremely harsh periods in our lives for potential to be developed.

Verily, verily, I say unto you, Except a corn of wheat fall into the ground and die, it abideth alone: but if it die, it bringeth forth much fruit (John 12:24 KJV).

Death connotes pain, and sacrifice of self-ambitions. It is saying, "Not my will, Lord, but yours be done." It is joining John the Baptist in saying, "Jesus must increase, and I must decrease" (John 3:30).

It is this dying part that most people do not like. However, we must realize that to be fruitful, we have to die first, just like a seed planted needs to die for germination to take place. Our fleshly desires have to die. Old ways of thinking have to die. Old habits have to be uprooted, and traditions have to go. All this is very painful. But without the old going away, the new cannot come in. In the process of dying, our resolve will be tested. This is where our patience is developed, and our endurance and perseverance is tested.

Dear brothers and sisters, when troubles come your way, consider it an opportunity for great joy (James 1:2 NLT).

Romans 5:3 says we should rejoice when we run into trouble. At the end of this seemingly difficult stage, if we pass this test of potential and character, we would come forth as pure gold. The only people with no problems are those who are dead.

But he knoweth the way that I take: when he hath tried me, I shall come forth as gold (Job 23:10 KJV).

The crucibles in which our character is tested and refined are problems and challenges. Fire will burn out every impurity in gold. The hotter the fire, the purer the gold. So the Bible encourages us to be thankful in those tough times, and look for Christ in the crisis, so we can come out stronger and purer to be used more by Him.

Now in a great house there are not only vessels of gold and silver but also of wood and clay, some for honorable use, some for

dishonorable. Therefore, if anyone cleanses himself from what is dishonorable, he will be a vessel for honorable use, set apart as holy, useful to the master of the house, ready for every good work (2 Timothy 2:20-21 NLT).

We should always see every adversity and challenge as an opportunity to grow and stretch. Sometimes, we would face adversities in life that are daunting. And if we analyze them purely from the intellectual point of view, we might end up in paralysis. Martin Luther King Jr. talked of "The paralysis of analysis."

I believe God lets us to go through some situations so that we can help others one day who find themselves in similar situations. Again, you must remember that it is never about you, but about the awesome things God wants to accomplish through you.

In Matthew 13:24-29, Jesus narrated the remarkable parable of the wheat and tares (weed). The parable is about a man who commissioned his servants to plant wheat. Whilst they slept at night, an enemy came and planted some weed seeds. After a while, the servants were perplexed when they saw the weeds, and wondered where they came from. Their master explained to them that the enemy had planted it. Immediately, they asked if they could go and pull out the weeds. The master prevented them from doing so. He explained to them that by taking out the weeds, they would pull out the wheat as well. The best course of action was to let both grow side by side, so the wheat might develop strong roots. When the time of harvest came, the weeds would be uprooted and burnt, whilst the wheat would be harvested and brought into the barn.

We learn from this story that adversity is the catalyst for

developing character and potential. Sometimes, we might forfeit the very opportunity to develop character by trying to squirm out of problems too soon. Instead of going around trying to explain to everyone how you have been wronged and criticized falsely, sometimes keeping quiet is the best thing to do. Jesus, instead of justifying Himself before His accusers, kept quiet. That, my friend, is dying.

Even though Jesus was God's Son, he learned obedience from the things he suffered (Hebrews 5:8 NLT).

Instead of being belligerent towards people who get on our nerves, we can learn patience, love, forgiveness, kindness, and other virtues that will allow us to reflect the glory of God. In the parable, we see good and evil growing side by side. Sometimes a lot of energy is wasted trying to answer critics and to justify ourselves to everyone. Sometimes we need to put on a smile, stand still, and see the salvation of the Lord.

To be promoted, we have to pass the test of potential and character. There are no shortcuts. Just as in school, if a person does not pass the exams, they have to repeat the exams.

Problems and adversities are opportunities in disguise. If you are jobless at the moment, it might be an opportunity to start your own business. See every challenge as a step to greatness. The greater the challenge, the greater the rewards. Goliath was David's access to greatness.

Every challenge reveals who we are, and shows us what areas of character and potential still need developing.

If thou faint in the day of adversity, thy strength is small (Proverbs 24:10 KJV).

Thank God that there is always grace to develop and become better, as long as we do not give up. It is not friends, but enemies that can help promote you and take you to the next level. It is not that which is comfortable, but that which is uncomfortable that brings the best out of you.

AND TO YOU I SAY, THIS GENERATION HAS NOT SEEN THE BEST OF YOU YET!

9

LEADERSHIP AND EXCELLENCE

"...I will make thee an eternal excellency, a joy of many generations" (Isaiah 60:15b KJV).

In this short chapter, I want to deal a little bit with leadership and excellence in a way I believe will be helpful. I'd like to offer a change of perspective.

Excellence is defined as the quality of being outstanding, or extremely good. Excellence is inseparable from leadership, for excellence is an integral part of leadership.

New generation leadership is excellence, and not lording over people. When I was in boarding school, one of the foremost criteria for selecting school prefects was to take into consideration their academic performance. It would not make sense to confer additional responsibilities on a person who is struggling with schoolwork. That would have been suicidal.

From the above Scripture, we can see that God wants us to not only be excellent, but to be an eternal excellency and a joy of many generations. This means that by our excellence, many generations will benefit from what we accomplish.

EXCELLENCE AND LOVE

To be excellent means to walk in love.

...And yet I will show you the most excellent way. ...If I speak in the tongues of men or of angels, but do not have love, I am only a resounding gong or a clanging cymbal (1 Corinthians 12:31; 13:1 NIV).

Loving God and loving others as you love yourself brings an aura on you that words cannot express.

He answered, "Love the Lord your God with all your heart and with all your soul and with all your strength and with all your mind"; and, "Love your neighbor as yourself" (Luke 10:27 KJV).

The golden rule is a derivative of this Scripture. When all is said and done, love is what will remain and never fail. It is the love of God that will triumph over all else. Two thousand years after Jesus died on the cross, His sacrifice of love is still winning the hearts of many. People do not really care what a person knows, until they know how much that person cares.

Loving God means acknowledging and celebrating our differences and uniqueness, and that of others. It is impossible to love others without loving ourselves first. Loving ourselves means accepting and celebrating the unique way God has designed us.

Loving God means obeying His commandments. *Jesus answered and said unto him, If a man love me, he will keep my words: and my Father will love him, and we will come unto him, and make our abode with him (John 14:23 KJV).*

LEADERSHIP

I believe God is calling everyone to be a leader. Everyone can develop leadership skills. Below are some characteristics of leaders.

Leadership is not a title; rather, it is being excellent and taking the lead in our field. Leadership is not about accolades, but it is doing something so well that no one could do it better. This is not considered a form of competition, but it is the expression of your uniqueness that displays the glory of God through you.

Leadership means following the cloud of God and not the crowd. Those who follow the cloud enter the Promised Land. Those who follow the crowd can easily perish in the wilderness of life.

Leadership is applying ourselves in our particular endeavors with all power and might, bringing all our abilities and resources to bear in the accomplishment of that thing.

Leadership is not lording over people, but being an example in all good things and loving people.

A leader is one who serves others. He that is greatest amongst you must be servant of all.

Leaders are sometimes persecuted for changing the culture and challenging tradition.

A leader is a reader. He who reads today will lead tomorrow. Those who sit around all day and "kill time" are far from being leaders. Reading places a man many years ahead of his contemporaries. I am not talking about reading to pass exams, but reading for self-development.

A leader is a person with a vision. A leader is a person of conviction. A leader is a person who is ready to die for a worthy cause. Nelson Mandela was willing to die for his cause. Martin Luther King Jr. was willing to die for what he believed. In most countries, people confuse politicians with leaders. Politicians have no conviction of their own, rather they do the biddings of those who would put them in power.

Leaders are creative people, always looking for ways to do things better, faster, and with more elegance. Leaders are people who have refused to abide by the status quo.

Sometimes, leaders are not seen in the public, but are the brains behind projects. Whenever a movie is running, those acting in the film are called the movie stars, but the real leaders are the movie directors, who may never be in the film nor known to the public.

We are all called to be leaders of excellence.

AND TO YOU I SAY, THIS GENERATION HAS NOT SEEN THE BEST OF YOU YET!

10

LEGACY

"A good man leaves an inheritance to his children's children, And the wealth of the sinner is stored up for the righteous" (Proverbs 13:22 NASB).

We live for the next generation. I heard my pastor say recently that we live for our children. I thought about the statement for a while. When I hear something for the first time, I tend to analyze it and put it under the scrutiny of the Word of God. As I pondered about that statement in the light of Scripture, I realized the truth it embodied.

Abraham was told by God that he was going to bless him. Abraham made it very clear to God that it was of no real value blessing him when he did not have a son to be heir.

And Abram said, "You have given me no children; so a servant in my household will be my heir" (Genesis 15:3 NIV).

God is the God of multiple generations. He is the God of Abraham, Isaac and Jacob (Matthew 22:32). There must be continuity. This means that in planning our lives, we must plan for at least three generations—Abraham-Isaac-Jacob, or our children's children. If we take a generation today to be thirty-five years, this means that the strategic life plan of each individual should span a minimum of 100 years.

When I finally got my bachelor's degree after many challenges, my dad told me he could now rest with his fathers, because he considered his job finished. The pride of most parents is tied to the success of their children.

What we do now with our lives is setting a precedence for generations yet unborn. Everything we do now is leaving a legacy, by default or design. Legacy can be positive or negative.

For example, a lot of diseases are genetically passed down from generations past. Sometimes, these diseases are introduced by family nutrition or generational cooking. For instance, some cultures are generally more susceptible to high blood pressure than others. This is no surprise, as the meals of these cultures are generally very spicy, and laden with too much fat used in cooking. Too much fat can line up inside of blood vessels and lead to high blood pressure.

One of the cultures that understand legacy are the Jews. The Jews keep a record of their family tree for centuries. They can easily trace back 20 generations of their ancestors. They understand the fact that they are products of past generations. It is rare in the Bible for a name to be mentioned in isolation.

When He began His ministry, Jesus Himself was about thirty years of age, being, as was supposed, the son of Joseph, the son of Eli, the son of Matthat, the son of Levi, the son of Melchi, the son of Jannai, the son of Joseph, the son of Mattathias, the son of Amos, the son of Nahum, the son of Hesli, the son of Naggai, the son of Maath, the son of Mattathias, the son of Semein, the son of Josech, the son of Joda, ... (Luke 3:23-26 NASB).

Now there was a certain man from Ramathaim-zophim from the hill country of Ephraim, and his name was Elkanah the son of Jeroham, the son of Elihu, the son of Tohu, the son of Zuph, an Ephraimite (I Samuel 1:1).

Past generations have a great impact on our destiny whether we like it or not. Understanding that will help us know what to avoid or emulate from past generations.

In Africa, there aren't such good records kept for most families. It is really difficult to trace the pedigree of many families with accuracy. Of course there is history that has been passed down through legends and folklore.

In the traditional African society and most Eastern cultures of old, it was critical to know where a person came from, especially when it came to marriage. Before a girl's hand was given in marriage, people were sent from the girl's village to go and study the culture of the groom's village. What kind of people were they? What were their values? Did they honor the marriage institution, or was divorce prevalent? Were they business-oriented, hard-working or lazy? Did they have a long or short life expectancy? Many of such questions were asked so they could ascertain the general trends and what to expect. Likewise, the groom's family would send its own people on the same expedition. Of course, times have changed, and people do not care for such things as much as before. However, they seem to understand that the blessings or the devils of past generations have a tendency to revisit future generations. Therefore, armed with such information, they would know what course to take.

Are you a man of multiple generations, or a person of one generation? Many nations are built without a forecast for the future. In many developing countries, leadership for the most part has been myopic. Many decisions are made without considering the impact they will have on generations yet unborn. Many decision are made based only on the present. The expression in Pidgin-English used in my dad's house for this is *chopbrokpotism.* It means that after a person has eaten a meal, he breaks the pot in which the meal was cooked, without thinking of the next meal.

One of the reasons why many people lag behind in wealth and development is because of the absence of the right legacy. It is God's will that we build on what former generations had built on. This will prevent re-inventing the wheel, so that future generations do not have to keep starting all over again.

The aftermath of war leaves buildings and infrastructures destroyed, and construction has to start from scratch. Money that would have been used for something else is being siphoned into building projects. Unfortunately, this has been the story of most

African countries.

I see a new generation of leaders that are rising up from the continent of Africa with a vision for one hundred to two hundred years, starting in the house of God.

Growing up in Africa, I was saddened to see many gigantic houses that had been left unfinished. I inquired why those mansions were not completed, and was told that the owner of the building died and upon their demise, there was no provision for the completion of the house. So these houses have been left desolate for many decades, with no one to complete them. Some of these houses and buildings have become hideouts for criminals. There are many people who have built a great empire of wealth, but at their demise, what they had taken years to build was reduced to rubble as the children fought over their inheritance, and destroyed each other in the process. Sometimes these people did not leave any will behind, therefore setting the stage for a civil war in their own house.

Will you leave behind an inheritance for your children's children? Or will they inherit debts from you?

A good man leaves an inheritance for his children's children. For you to leave an inheritance for your children's children, you've got to have enough. We live in a generation where many leave behind debts to their children.

2 Kings 4 talks about the story of a prophet who died in debt, with the kids as collateral. So the creditors came to take the kids away and the wife cried unto the prophet Elisha for help. What an ordeal! What a heart-wrenching scenario! The death of a man became a curse to his posterity because he left the wrong legacy. This is no strange scenario, even in certain parts of the world today. I was once told a case of a man who died in debt, and his 16-year-old daughter was given to the 60-year-old creditor for marriage, as settlement for the debt.

When I go to funerals, I am very cognizant of the fact that people are crying for different reasons. At one funeral, where a pilot had died in a plane crash, one woman was crying profusely, almost wailing. It turned out that the deceased owed her a large sum of money, which she was not sure how to get back.

When we die, it should bring about tears of joy and celebration for a life fully lived, and not cries of anguish because of the suffering that will ensue.

May your kids not inherit debts, but wealth, in Jesus' name. I watched an old clip of a comedian who said he would leave debts as an inheritance for his kids, since it took him a lot of time and energy to accumulate.

Taking stock of what you are doing presently, do you honestly think you will be able to leave an inheritance for your children's children?

However, our legacy should not be limited to our children only, but to our nation and to our world. "Ask not what your country can do for you; ask what you can do for your country." John F. Kennedy.

Below are some areas we should work on to leave a legacy.

SPIRITUAL

By obeying God and living by faith, we leave a legacy that inspires future generations.

By faith these people overthrew kingdoms, ruled with justice, and received what God had promised them. They shut the mouths of lions (Hebrews 11:33. NLT).

We should leave a godly legacy. We should teach our children to love God.

For I have chosen him, so that he will direct his children and his household after him to keep the way of the LORD by doing what is right and just, so that the LORD will bring about for Abraham what he has promised him (Genesis 18:19 NIV).

Abraham was chosen by God because he would teach his children to love God.

It is important to not pass down ungodly religion, but a godly legacy. We are not to pass down some of the ungodly traditions of our forefathers. Of recent, my family had to deal with some of those traditions that make the word of God of none effect.

...thus making void the word of God by your tradition that you have handed down... (Mark 7:13 ESV).

In my village, almost every family has a cup that has been passed down from different generations. The heir of that family is normally the custodian of the cup. At special ceremonies, such as weddings, the main people of the occasion are expected to drink from this "cup of blessing" as many words are pronounced and libations are poured. The only problem is that not many family members know where that cup originated from, nor what covenants are tied with that cup. They are not aware of how those covenants play out in people's lives. In my family my dad, being the head of the family, has been the custodian of that cup. We had to get a pastor to dethrone him as heir of past traditions, and enthrone him as head of the family with a Bible. So when my dad is handing over blessings to the next generation, he will be handing blessings based on the blessings of Abraham.

That the blessing of Abraham might come on the Gentiles through Jesus Christ; that we might receive the promise of the Spirit through faith (Galatians 3:14 KJV).

Henceforth, the blessings my dad will hand down to the next generation will be based on the promises of God and on the blood of Jesus. That speaks better things than the blood of Abel.

Some people have tribal marks that are tied to certain deities. Some of this stuff can have a grave impact on a person's destiny. Thank

God for deliverance in Christ Jesus. In the name of Jesus, I break any negative covenants in your life established through all such marks.

My dear friend, do not let your destiny be tied to some ancient family god and think it is okay. Your identity should be in Christ and Christ alone, and you should pass down a godly legacy.

FINANCIAL AND ECONOMIC LEGACY

Economically, most generations start from scratch because there was nothing left to build on. There are many challenges which we, as a people from Africa, have to overcome in the coming years.

Africa as a continent is very young, and we take into consideration the many displacements that have taken place during the era of slave trade and colonialism.

However, we have to move on and not get stuck in the past. I have seen many wealthy people who died, and within a period of a year their family lost everything they had so labored for during their lifetime.

Some challenges of leaving a financial legacy.

- **Lack of systems.** The greatest problem in having a financial and economy legacy has been the lack of systems. In the western hemisphere, institutions and companies easily last many generations after the founder died because they have systems for continuity in place. McDonald's, Coca Cola, and many more have outlived their founders and are growing by leaps and bounds. In 2011, Steve Jobs, the co-founder of Apple, passed away. In spite of that, Apple is growing stronger every day because it was not built around an individual but on systems that have continuity wired in them.

In Africa, most companies and institutions die with their founder. Most of these companies are built around individuals. Generally, these individuals do not prepare for their death. So when death strikes, most people do not know who to go to, since the go-to person is no longer alive. This has to change for there to be a legacy.

- **Trying to get people to do what they are not called nor gifted to do**. People try to force their kids to continue running their businesses without necessarily finding out if the kids really want to do it. Family businesses do well, but one of the greatest gifts given to man is choice. If a child is trained to do something he or she does not want and like doing, it is just a matter of time. They can do it for a while when the parents are still alive, but once the parent is dead, they will naturally gravitate to what they always wanted to do. Your children can be beneficiaries of your wealth without being directly involved in the management of your assets.

Leave a financial legacy to your family and community. This can be achieved through businesses, foundations, and intellectual properties, trust funds, etc. Many people have composed songs that are still getting royalties many decades after their death. Their children and grandchildren are reaping the benefits of the creativity of grandpa and grandma.

BLESSING

That is the main legacy we need to leave. Blessing the next generation to be better than us. Blessings can take the form of teaching and imparting knowledge, or speaking prophetic words to them. This kind of legacy is what Abraham passed on to Isaac, and Isaac transferred to Jacob. To bless someone is to empower that person to prosper and succeed in all they do. I remember visiting

Cameroon in 2008, and as I said before, my father has not been doing very well health-wise for about a decade. So when he saw me he was very ecstatic, and told me he was never sure he would see me again. He asked me to kneel down and he blessed me in the name of the Lord. What a glorious moment that was to me.

TRANSFER OF KNOWLEDGE

A legacy of knowledge can be left through books, inventions, systems, etc. A friend told me of a man in Cameroon dubbed "Pa Headache." The man was given the title because of his ability to cure chronic headaches by massaging certain veins at the back of a person's neck. Such knowledge could be lost if he does not transfer it to the next generation. We still read the books of people long dead and we are blessed and empowered by their writings. I wonder what knowledge you could transfer to the next generation by writing a book.

INFRASTRUCTURE

Buildings can be built that will last for centuries. In Cameroon, Germans left a legacy by the infrastructures they constructed. After over a century, those buildings are still standing strong.

In life we can either be part of a problem, or part of a solution. By leaving the right legacy, we are becoming part of the solution for future generations.

AND TO YOU I SAY, THIS GENERATION HAS NOT SEEN THE BEST OF YOU YET!

11

START NOW

He who observes the wind [and waits for all conditions to be favourable] will not sow, and he who regards the clouds will not reap (Ecclesiastes 11:4 AMP).

It has been proven scientifically that successful people, and those who achieve their dreams, make decisions fast and change their minds slowly. On the other hand, those who fail usually take a long time to reach a decision, if ever, then change their mind very often.

I know a couple of great leaders that fall under the first category. When they get inspired, they make a phone call immediately for someone to take action and make it happen. They do not wait and hope that they will remember later. One of them is Pastor Mel Mullen, my current senior pastor and founder of Word of Life Church. Another person I am closely acquainted with through books is Bishop Dag Heward-Mills of Light House Chapel International. The great achievements of these leaders are a testimony of their fast decision making abilities. Once they learn something or see something that ties in with their vision, they immediately take action to see it accomplished.

That is how businesses get started. That is how dreams are fulfilled. And that is how a small thing can make a big difference as a result of action being taken. That is why some people do in a day what would take a year for others to do. Whilst others are *"religiously praying about it,"* seeking the advice from all and sundry, leaders and achievers take action immediately. This is not discounting the importance of seeking advice.

You must make a decision to start right away if you ever want to fulfil your dream. Because the only time we really have is now.

Tomorrow is promised to no man. There is certainly something small you could start now that would take you to your destination. Success has been described not only as a destination, but as a journey. If you are taking steps towards your goal, then you are succeeding to a certain degree.

Time and tides do not wait for any person. Opportunities are delivered on the conveyor belt of time. We either pick them up or let them go by.

Starting now means giving your life to Jesus now. Many people do not attend to the most important aspect of their life—their eternal destiny. For today is the day of salvation, and now is the time when the gates of salvation have been swung wide open.

It has been said that the road to hell is paved with good intentions. Edward Irvin said, "Procrastination is the kidnapper of souls and the recruiter of hell." Sometimes delaying might turn into permanent denial. Most people say, "When I get older, I will think about giving my life to God and serving Him." However, the Word of God admonishes us to serve God in the days of our youth, for in old age, the physical strength required to do the work of God may not be available. Sometimes tomorrow might never come. Today is the day the Lord has made, let us rejoice and be glad in it (Psalm 118:24).

I have spoken to many people who claim they do not believe there is God. However, they admit at one time in their lives, they felt the presence of God. Delaying the acceptance of God's call leads to a hardened heart with the passage of time. The best time to commit one's life to Jesus is when a person is young. Young people have just one problem; youthful lust. Generally people become bitter, resentful, cynical, and untrusting as they get older. Many adults have lived long enough to witness the evil in this world. They have been betrayed and rejected. All these make them question the existence of God. Therefore, believe in Jesus now and make Him your Lord and Savior now, for tomorrow might be too late.

There are things which you need to start now or you might never do them. Circumstances might never be right for you to do them. You might never have the money to invest at a large scale, but you can start small.

Take a minute to reflect on all the great ideas that you've had in the past and planned to start something. Years later, you have not done anything about them.

At the beginning of the year, I set out to give a certain percentage of my income to the gospel and to humanitarian causes, once I have made a certain amount of money. Whilst reading the book *The Blessed Life* by Robert Morris, I was reminded by the passage below;

Now He who supplies seed to the sower and bread for food will supply and multiply your seed for sowing and increase the harvest of your righteousness (11 Corinthians 9:10 KJV).

So I called my wife and asked her to agree with me to start giving a set amount immediately. I believe we are living in a season where God is redeeming time, and only those who are fast to act will work in his plan. As you grow older, the more you come to terms with the fact that "time and tide wait for nobody."

Start moving in the direction of your present knowledge and ability towards your goal. You do not have to know everything about everything before you start moving. Start shining the little light you have to the world.

Yes, start now. If you want to get into business, start now by buying books on setting up a business, how to finance a business, how to register a business, what makes a business fail or succeed. Start getting the knowledge in preparation for launching. Someone said it is better to be prepared and no opportunities come than for opportunities to come and you are not prepared. I had an awesome opportunity once to have a business contract of over half a million dollars a year in income. I was not prepared for it, and out of integrity I had to say no.

I once read of an incredible story which I will attempt to narrate as much as I can remember. A man once undertook a long journey on foot through the forest that was to last many hours. Eventually, darkness overtook him, but because he was travelling through the jungle, he was determined not to spend the night on the way. In time, he came across a bag that was full of what seemed like pebbles. So he picked up the bag and by this time, he was walking along a river bank. In order to distract potential predators and stay awake, he opened the bag and started throwing away the pebbles into the river. Finally, when he arrived at his destination, only a few of those pebbles were left. So he decided to examine what kind of pebbles were in the bag. To his uttermost surprise, he discovered that he had been throwing away diamonds. This is an example of wasting one of the most precious gifts given to us by God—time. A person can get to the end of his life and realize he has thrown away all the time he had through procrastination, indecision, and doing the wrong things.

Doors will not always be open. Therefore, when a door opens to do something, it is important to seize the moment. There will never be a perfect condition or circumstance to do all that one needs to do. We must walk by faith, even when we do not understand it all or do not have all the answers.

The future is not deferred to a future date. The future is now. Jesus once made a remarkable statement. He said, "The hour is coming, now is that time, when true worshippers of God will worship Him in spirit and in truth" (John 4:23). It would appear it meant the hour was deferred in some future dispensation, but then He qualified the statement by explaining that time as now. Our entire future is predicated on what we do now. Like Mike Murdock so aptly captured it, "Our future is hidden in our daily routine." Therefore, what we do now becomes seeds that determine the harvest of tomorrow. Starting now means giving attention to your intentions now. So, my dear friend, start now.

AND TO YOU I SAY, THIS GENERATION HAS NOT SEEN THE BEST OF YOU YET!

12

FINISHING WELL

I have fought the good fight, I have finished the race, I have kept the faith (2 Timothy 4:7 NIV).

In the parable of the sower, there are four different kinds of soil in which the seeds were sown (Matthew 13:1-23). Of the four types of soil, only one soil yielded fruit. In these verses, we see that the problem was not the seed or potential, but the kind of soil in which the seeds were put.

In the first case, the soil was the roadside on which the seeds fell, and the birds of the air came and immediately ate them. The first soil clearly rejected the seed. The first soil represents those who refuse the call of God, reject knowledge and everything that has to do with them fulfilling God's purpose for their lives. The first soil represents those who have a very casual attitude towards life. This group consists of people who do not know what is happening, and do not really seem to care. So this group poses no challenge to the devil when he comes to destroy their lives and purpose. In a sense, this group assists him in destroying them through their indifference; their lethargic, apathetic, and evasive attitude towards life. From the onset, this group does not even get started, and therefore does not count, as only that which got started can be finished.

However, within the context of finishing well, the real tragedy are the two subsequent soil types. These groups accepted the message and had a vision. The seed was planted, and the vision started growing. Everyone could see the potential. However, somewhere along the pipeline, challenges came; the cares of this world distracted them. The things of this world became very attractive to them and they soon lost focus. They could not produce any fruit at the end. This is the story of those who do not pay the price to finish well.

In the parable of the ten virgins, five made it to the banquet and five did not (Matthew 25:1-13). The main difference that separated the two groups was the extra oil. They were all virgins, they were all dressed up, they all had lamps, but the foolish virgins took just enough oil, whilst the wise virgins took extra oil. To finish well, a person needs to do more than enough, and go the extra mile. Doing just enough is not enough. In every arena, be it spiritual, physical or intellectual, enough will never be enough. It is the extra miles, extra prayers, extra studying, extra investment, extra sacrifice, extra work, extra training, extra loving and kindness that takes a man and a woman across the finishing line.

I press toward the mark for the prize of the high calling of God in Christ Jesus (Philippians 3:14 KJV).

Paul the apostle had to press towards the mark for the prize of the high calling. Because our calling is high, the prize to be received is high, and the price to be paid is equally high.

To finish well means to stay on the course to the very end. As we get older, we should never retire. We can change roles due to the aging process taking its toll and slowing us up a little bit; however, to retire completely and sit idly doing nothing is opening the door for confusion.

Statistics have shown that those who retire completely from work die within 2–5 years. This is because the signal is given to the body that there is nothing to really live for any more.

Finishing well might mean not retiring, but rather to keep re-firing. For those who think it might be over, you never know what you are still capable of doing at a certain stage of your life. Let me use the story below to explain this more.

Before the year 1990, the name Cameroon did not mean anything to most non-Africans. But after the 1990 Football world cup in

Italy, Cameroon was put on the world map, thanks to the qualification and brilliant performance by the indomitable Lions of Cameroon (the Cameroon national football team) at the FIFA World Cup. Most especially thanks to the legendary football skills of Roger Milla. In most of the countries I have been to, Cameroon is mainly remembered by football (soccer), referenced to Roger Milla and his trademark dance at *Italia 90*.

Roger Milla is a glaring testimony to the fact that no one should ever retire, but keep re-firing, no matter the age. This iconic figure had retired from football, and a grandiose jubilee celebration had been organized to commemorate the end of an excellent football career.

However, when Cameroon qualified for the FIFA World Cup of 1990, Milla was fished out of retirement at the age of 38 by presidential decree and brought back onto the center stage of world football to defend his country. The rest is now history.

Milla goes down in history as the oldest man to have scored a goal in a world cup final, at the age of 42, for he also represented Cameroon at the FIFA World Cup of 1994 and scored a goal.

It might appear as though you have withered into insignificance, but I encourage you to keep believing and keep dreaming and keep working. One of these days, an opportunity will show up, and by divine decree and providence, you will be summoned out of hiding to make a lasting mark on the world and leave an indelible legacy. So never retire, but keep re-firing!

To finish well means knowing what role you ought to be playing at every stage of your life. King David was a man after God's heart— because of his love for God. However, David's greatest mistakes of his life were those of timing. When he committed adultery with Bathsheba, it was a time when kings went to war, and he was supposed to be at war. However, Mr. Man was at home relaxing on the rooftop when suddenly he saw a naked woman bathing and eventually slept with her (2 Samuel 11:1-5). When David was much older, it was time for him to stay at home and give directions. However, he found himself at the warfront, behind enemy lines, and almost got killed because of that. It almost caused him to not finish well (2 Samuel 21:16-17). If Satan cannot stop a person, he will push that individual until he wears out. If he cannot convince a person to be lazy and "rust," he will push that individual to ride so fast until he or she runs out of breath and burns out. Surely, timing is everything.

Finishing well means being watchful to the very end. The diminishing strength of old age sometimes affects the mind of people and blurs their judgment. Sometimes, convictions are compromised. Many great men have fallen in some form of scandal because they were not watchful till the very end.

You were running a good race. Who cut in on you to keep you from obeying the truth (Galatians 5:7 NIV)?

After Jesus overcame Satan's temptation in the wilderness, Satan went away for a season. Satan only goes away for a season. Be sure he is coming back. Satan later came back many times, and even tried to use Peter to stop Jesus from dying on the cross. Jesus had to say "Get thee behind me Satan…" Therefore it is critical to be watchful and vigilant all the time, and not take things for granted.

Be sober, be vigilant; because your adversary the devil walks about like a roaring lion, seeking whom he may devour (1 Peter 5:8 NKJV).

Finishing well means preparing for the long haul. The devil never gives up. He will always keep trying to attack us in areas where he sees weakness. Therefore, we ought to fight to the very end. Satan never tempts people at their point of strength, but at their point of weakness. He watches people from birth, and studies their weaknesses to see where they are more vulnerable and prone to fall. Then he makes sure he keeps attacking that weakness link with temptations. James says a man is tempted when he is enticed by his own lust (James 1:14).

The end of a matter is better than its beginning, and patience is better than pride (Ecclesiastes 7:8 KJV).

To finish well, we must keep our eyes on the prize of the high calling, and keep pressing on until the very end. Your calling is not an ordinary kind of calling; it is a high and divine calling.

I press toward the mark for the prize of the high calling of God in Christ Jesus (Philippians 4:13 KJV).

To finish well, we must be able to endure challenges and seasons of hardship.

...who for the joy that was set before him endured the cross, despising the shame, and is set down at the right hand of the throne of God (Hebrews 12:2 KJV).

One of the traits of those who succeed in a significant way is the ability to stand undefeated in periods of hardship. Life is not always easy. Challenges are the litmus tests used by life to determine who stays in the race and who gets eliminated. Therefore, arm yourself with the knowledge that tough times will come. But knowledge and willpower are not what will ultimately make a man stand. The only thing that will make a man stand is the Word of God. Adhering to and practicing the Word of God will make a man stand forever (1 John 2:17). For whosoever builds on the Word of God is like a man building on the rock; when the winds of life come that person is unshakable (Matthew 7:24-27). Building one's life on anything other than on God's Word might seem to stand for a while, but eventually it will fall apart. Any high-sounding idea or philosophy that is not in sync with the Word of God has an expiry date. Only the Word of God and those who practice it live for ever

Finishing well means surrounding ourselves with the right people till the very end. It can be lethal sometimes to move away from people who have been loyal to you and get close to those who might want to use you. Many have done that at the end of their lives and caused a lot of confusion and pain to those loyal to them.

In some cases, they had no legacy or continuation of their work, as they had hurt all those who would have continued it.

Finishing well means dealing radically and completely with things that can take you out of the race. These include petty sins that are tolerated as weaknesses. Whilst it is true that sometimes we do have negative things in our lives we are struggling to overcome, it is also true that sometimes people are not willing to part with certain sins they enjoy committing. These are the little foxes that can spoil the vine (Songs of Solomon 2:15). I told one individual that we are to resist temptation and not enjoy it. He told me that there are times when he had enjoyed temptation, especially sexual temptation to sin. May God help us!

Finishing well means overcoming certain sins in the day of strength. King Saul was commanded to destroy the Amalekites and annihilate them. God had empowered him with the strength to carry out that command. He did not obey that command, and was later killed by an Amalekite when he was weak. "I am an Amalekite" was the bold declaration by the young man who killed Saul (2 Kings 1:8). What a person does not overcome in his day of strength can overcome him in the day of weakness.

Finishing well means obeying God, even when it does not make sense. God knows all of the future, and we do not. It is therefore critical to walk by faith and obey God, even when it does not make logical sense. As seen above, King Saul was commanded by God to annihilate the Amalekites. The main reason was that God wanted to judge them for the manner in which they had treated the Israelites on their way out of Egypt (1 Samuel 15:3). God had also seen the danger the Amalekites would pose to Israel in the future. King Saul disobeyed the command to completely destroy them, and it was an Amalekite that killed him at the end. Solomon was commanded not to get married to women outside of Israel who could lure him to worship idols. He did not obey that command and got married to many of these strange women, who caused him to stray away from God. Many times, people wish they had obeyed a command from God, or adhered to an advice from a dad as they look back and see the consequences of their disobedience.

Finishing well means looking forward to the coming of Jesus whilst being busy. There is something about looking forward to the return of Jesus that makes a person make quality decisions—decisions that take into account eternal rewards and consequences.

Finally, finishing well is hearing those sweet, juicy, priceless, wonderful, unparalleled, stupendous, and humbling words from the Master, Jesus, as he says to you:

"... Well done, thou good and faithful servant: thou hast been faithful over a few things, I will make thee ruler over many things: enter thou into the joy of thy lord."

AND TO YOU I SAY, THIS GENERATION HAS NOT SEEN THE BEST OF YOU YET!

SECTION
2

THE AFRICAN ENTREPRENEUR

INTRODUCTION

As seen in the introduction of this book, most Africans were entrepreneurs before African colonization. (Again, this is not an indictment of colonialism, nor is it any excuse for Africans not moving forward.) Africans were traders. Some reared cattle and sheep, and some were farmers who sold their products or bartered them at different markets. Simply put, Africans were entrepreneurs in their own right. Colonization made the concept of jobs as a means of a secured financial future very popular. Having a business was considered risky and uncertain. In due season, most people bought into this concept. People aspired to go to school or go through some professional course and get a degree or diploma. The next step was to seek employment with the government, which at the time was one of the highest employers.

Dressed in suits and ties like the colonial masters, and having a position and a title to go with it became the pride of many. Today, the dream of most Africans is to become an employee and not an employer. Could it be that one of the greatest losses to Africans in the aftermath of colonialism is the loss of the *entrepreneurial spirit*?

Growing up in Cameroon, I never heard a parent being proud of the fact that their child was a businessperson or investor. Rather, parents were proud to announce to their friends: "This is my son, who is a doctor," or "This is my daughter, who is a pharmacist." It spells out the fact that they are educated, even if they have no money to their name. This has created a culture in which most people are now interested in titles and the respect attached with these titles instead of developing their potential to bring value to the market place. Here are some examples of people I know who took the bold step to start their own businesses.

A friend of mine from Cameroon with whom I attended university in the UK had finished his degree in computer designing. Upon completion, he could not get a job in his field, and worked in a factory for over a year. I met him one day shortly before I relocated to Canada in 2011 and he made an incredible statement. He said, "Godlove, I will never search for a job again." So I wanted to know why. He went on to tell me how he had struggled for over a year working in a factory with a degree in his pocket. Eventually, someone asked him to start his own business. He resisted for a while, and thought he could never do it. Fear and lack of confidence incapacitated him for a while. Eventually, he finally heeded to the idea and started his own business. He told me that in the first month, he made 3,000 pounds; the second month, he made 10,000 pounds. The average monthly wage for a graduate in the UK is in the neighborhood of 2,500 pounds a month. It is with this backdrop that he said he will never look for a job again. If he could do it, you can do it.

There is another African who studied nursing in the UK. He was in the process of doing a PhD in nursing when he eventually had an idea to become an entrepreneur, specializing in bringing immigrants into the country to work. Within a short period of time, he became a very wealthy man. I met him at a fundraising event and he shared how he had sold one of his houses and given all the money to his home church that was involved in a building project at the time.

The third example of someone I know who got into business was a friend of mine in Germany called Don. I met him in church when I was a student and he was gainfully employed. One Saturday, he asked me to accompany him to a computer trade fair somewhere around the city of Heidelberg. He told me he had quit his job and wanted to start his own business in selling refurbished computers and computer accessories. So he took a few desktop monitors along with him, which we sold. At the end, he handed me a 50 Euro bill as compensation for working with him. After that day, he asked me a couple of times if I could go with him to sell computers, but I could not accompany him since I was busy on Saturdays. A year later, he invited me to his office and warehouse, where he had all his stock of computers. It was then that I had one of the greatest shocks of my life. He had rented a large space of over 5,000 square feet, all filled with computers and accessories. He had three employees working for him. They travelled all over Europe selling computers at different trade fairs. I was able to accompany him to Amsterdam to one of these trade fairs.

I could not believe what he had accomplished within a year by stepping out in faith to fulfil his dream as an entrepreneur. He was making a lot of money, and was also a great giver. From time to time he would give me a *holy handshake*, a handshake when someone greets you with money in their palm for you.

13

GOD AND BUSINESS

As they heard these things, he proceeded to tell a parable, because he was near to Jerusalem, and because they supposed that the kingdom of God was to appear immediately. He said therefore, "A nobleman went into a far country to receive for himself a kingdom and then return. Calling ten of his servants, he gave them ten minas, and said to them, 'Engage in business until I come.' But his citizens hated him and sent a delegation after him, saying, 'We do not want this man to reign over us.' When he returned, having received the kingdom, he ordered these servants to whom he had given the money to be called to him, that he might know what they had gained by doing business. The first came before him, saying, 'Lord, your mina has made ten minas more.' And he said to him, 'Well done, good servant! Because you have been faithful in a very little, you shall have authority over ten cities.' And the second came, saying, 'Lord, your mina has made five minas.' And he said to him, 'And you are to be over five cities.' Then another came, saying, 'Lord, here is your mina, which I kept laid away in a handkerchief; for I was afraid of you, because you are a severe man. You take what you did not deposit, and reap what you did not sow.' He said to him, 'I will condemn you with your own words, you wicked servant! You knew that I was a severe man, taking what I did not deposit and reaping what I did not sow? Why then did you not put my money in the bank, and at my coming I might have collected it with interest?' And he said to those who stood by, 'Take the mina from him, and give it to the one who has the ten minas.' And they said to him, 'Lord, he has ten minas!', 'I tell you that to everyone who has, more will be given, but from the one who has not, even what he has will be taken away.

In the parable of the talent, we see the premise on which Jesus based this parable.

Many people have folded their arms and instead of being

productive, sit idly waiting for the kingdom of God to come. Many well-intentioned people have taken the coming of Jesus out of context. Instead of being industrious and entrepreneurial, they have put themselves in a state of limbo. People have had opportunities to invest and buy land, but they refused to seize these opportunities with the excuse that Jesus is coming soon, and there is no time to focus on earthly things.

Some churches have turned down opportunities to buy land and build a church building. They preferred to rent, enriching landlords as they waited for the return of Jesus. However, Jesus said we should occupy ourselves until he comes back. Other translations of the Bible use "invest" or "do business until I come."

It is quite interesting that throughout the Word of God, many references are made about business. Below are some examples.

- *And he said unto them, How is it that ye sought me? wist ye not that I **must** be about my Father's **business** (Luke 2:49 KJV)?*

- *Calling ten of his servants, he gave them ten minas, and said to them, 'Engage in business until I come' (Luke 19:13 ESV).*

- *Thus says the LORD, your Redeemer, the Holy One of Israel: "I am the LORD your God, who teaches you to profit, who leads you in the way you should go" (Isaiah 48:17 ESV).*

The question is, what and whose business are you in?

Until we grasp the fact that business is at the very core of God's will and purpose for man, we would go through life with a *laissez-faire* attitude and be unproductive and unfruitful in all that we do.

When you grasp this concept and get a revelation of your very life being a business, it would revolutionize everything you do, how you do it, and the excellence and urgency with which you do it.

In the very creation of man, God created man with business in His mind.

*Then God said, "Let Us make man in Our image, according to Our likeness; and let them rule over the fish of the sea and over the birds of the sky and over the cattle and over all the earth, and over every creeping thing that creeps on the earth." God created man in His own image, in the image of God He created him; male and female He created them. God **blessed** them; and God said to them, "Be **fruitful** and **multiply**, and **fill** the earth, and subdue it; and rule over the fish of the sea and over the birds of the sky and over every living thing that moves on the earth" (Genesis 1:26-28 NIV).*

At the core of every business is the goal for multiplication, fruitfulness, profit, gain, expansion and filling of the earth.

Every business that is doing extremely well today and has become a global phenomenon is fulfilling all these requirements to some extent. McDonald's is fruitful, multiplying and filling every corner of the earth. Burger King, Coca Cola, Apple, and Microsoft are all fruitful, multiplying and filling the earth. You can hardly go anywhere in the world without seeing a trace of Coca Cola or any of the above-mentioned institutions.

Thus saith the LORD, thy Redeemer, the Holy One of Israel; I am the LORD thy God which <u>teacheth thee to profit</u>, which leadeth thee by the way that thou shouldest go (Isaiah 48:17 KJV).

Everything thing God mandated man to do and accomplish was intended to be a business. For instance, church is the business of expanding the kingdom of God on the earth through the winning of souls and filling the whole earth with believers. That is what is normally called the great commission.

For the earth shall be <u>filled</u> with the knowledge of the glory of the LORD, as the waters cover the sea (Habakkuk 2:14 KJV).

And he said unto them, <u>Go ye into all the world,</u> and preach the gospel to every creature. He that believeth and is baptized shall be *saved; but he that believeth not shall be damned (Mark 16:15-16. KJV).*

This means that everything we have succeeded in and are succeeding in is because it was and is being treated as a business. Marriages that succeed and thrive are marriages that are treated as a business.

Churches that succeed and have a lasting impact after many centuries are churches that are being handled as a business.

Every business starts with a strategic plan which includes, but is not limited to the following:

- Vision: The future. Write it down.

- Mission: Purpose. Write it down.

- Core Values: What the business stand for.

- Strategic Areas of Focus: Long-term areas of focus.

- Strategic Goals: Long-term goals.

- Action Plans: Steps taken to accomplish goals.

Let us look at the main pillars of every business.

Accounting department: Every organization, institution, and marriage has an accounting department or it will collapse. Jesus' ministry had an accounting department with Judas Iscariot at the helm of it. Many books have been written on the subject of accounting.

Financing department: Every business and organization has a financing department, be it from donors, equity, shareholders, or loans, etc. The Bible says that *"...money answers all things" (Ecclesiastes 10:19).*

Human resource department: This department galvanizes and optimizes the gifts, skills and abilities of the workers, and channels them towards the accomplishment of corporate goals and objectives.

Marketing department: The department that advertises the goals, products and services of the organization. In church lingo, this is called evangelizing, with Jesus as the "Product."

In our personal lives, it is obvious to see that it has to be handled as a business. A person might be a sole proprietor or have a business with no overhead. In this case, one person may handle all these areas; yet all have to be handled well for any form of productivity to take place.

R&D or research and development department: The creative department, where the innovation machinery is at work.

Why entrepreneurship?

1. It is one of the keys to world evangelism. The gospel is free, but it is very expensive to propagate it. Through entrepreneurship, financial resources are created to give to the preaching of the gospel. One of the most effective ways of preaching the gospel in these last days is through television and radio. Media are very expensive to finance. Organising mass crusades sometimes costs millions of dollars. Many pastors and ministers have quit preaching because they could not make ends meet, as their first commitment is to look after their family. A couple of years ago, whilst in Germany, the pastor of the church I attended had to give monthly allowances to a group of pastors in a developing country. These pastors had quit preaching the gospel and went back to work full-time because they could not take care of their families from preaching alone. In

some places, pastors can work and pastor a church at the same time. In other places, either the jobs are difficult to come by, or ministers of the gospel are not permitted to work. There is therefore the need to send money to pastors or missionaries to meet their needs so they can be more effective in evangelising.

How, then, can they call on the one they have not believed in? And how then can they believe in the one of whom they have not heard? And how can they hear without someone preaching to them? **And how can anyone preach unless they are sent?** *As it is written: "How beautiful are the feet of those who bring good news" (Romans 10:14-15 NIV).*

2. Someone in business is more likely to fulfil their purpose than someone working at a job for all their life. It is difficult to fulfil your purpose working at a job all your life. It is okay to start out working at a job. However, to work for 30–40 years for a company with a few weeks of holidays each year makes it difficult to have time to do the things you have been called to do. Most people are looking forward to retirement, when they would have time to travel and know the world and reach out to their world. This is very presumptuous, as most people retire when they are already tired. Due to the mutuality of life, it is important to help people fulfil their dreams, but it should never be at the cost of fulfilling your own dreams.

One day someone told me, "If you do not fulfil your dreams, you will help fulfil those of others." I went to work later that day and I overheard two guys talking about dreams. I called one of them and asked them what they were talking about, and he made the same statement I had been told earlier on. That was a God moment for me.

I must add here that you should never quit your job and get into business without having a residual fund for the period of transition, unless you know what you are doing. Do not let the family suffer because of lack of wisdom. Generally, it is better to start a business whilst working and do both side by side until the business picks up momentum before quitting the job.

3. It is one of the greatest keys to financial freedom. Recently I was having a conversation with a friend who has a fairly good and secure job that comes with great benefits. The only problem is that his salary has been capped. He is earning the highest he can earn in his organisation in a non-management position. To earn higher, he would need to switch to a managerial position and accept all the pressure that comes with it, or look for a new organisation to work for. A job can greatly limit your earning capacity. In a business, a man can net in a day what would take three years to earn at a job. I heard someone say that he once earned in an hour more than what his dad earned in a lifetime working for the army.

If your future is tied to writing resumes, you might really be in trouble. Writing resumes can really be frustrating. I know of one man who is worth millions of dollars whose life was radically changed when he had this revelation. He had travelled from the UK to the USA with a wonderful resume, desperate to get a great job. Whilst in America, someone asked him how his future could depend on a resume. That statement so transformed him, to the extent that he started his own business. The last time I heard him talk in 2011, his business was worth over nine million US dollars. Take your future in your hands and start your own business, and do not let someone in an office somewhere determine how far you can go in life by deciding whether to employ you or not.

4. With a business, one has the potential to earn limitless amounts of money to help the poor and give to the gospel. I came home today and switched on the TV and I was touched by the organisation *Operation Smile*, which offers free operations to kids who are born with cleft lips. I was heartbroken to see a lot of kids turned down from this operation since everything is contingent on the funding available. You see, there are many people destitute and in dire need for help. But with a salary, people can barely support themselves and help relatives, never mind giving to others. You cannot give what you do not have.

The Bill and Melinda Gates foundation has given over 2.5 billion dollars in grants to help provide free HIV medication in Africa. This would never have been possible if Mr. Gates was at a 9–5 job.

To have the impact we need to have on our planet, we need to get into business.

5. Those with businesses generally have more time to spend with their families and to do the things they want to do in life, and also enjoy life.

I have friend who is in the food technology industry and had a tough time securing employment in the city where he lived with his family. Due to circumstances, it was best for his wife to maintain her job in the town where they lived. Therefore, for well over four years he lived and worked in other cities, and travelled once every fortnight to be with his family. About a year ago he got fed up with this lifestyle and decided to quit his job and his ambition to do a PhD. He started his own consultancy to help small businesses gain a competitive advantage in the marketplace. He recently wrote on one of his blogs that he is yet to experience a month that he earns less being self-employed than what he earned when he was employed as a manager. He has been able to buy his own home, and the vehicle he desired for his family. These are things he might not have easily accomplished with the earnings from his job. Now he stays at home and spends more time with his family. Until you become tired and fed up with the life of mediocrity and being driven by circumstances, you will stay at the same place of your life. What we tolerate, we can never change.

6. Those with their own business are more flexible with their time and have more control over their schedules. I have a friend who owns a business and can easily leave work at any time to pick up his children from daycare or school. With a job, the story is quite different, as one needs to ask permission all the time and risk being fired.

7. Having a business gives a person the time to attend to family issues and be there for family members when needed. When a friend of mind lost his father, he was able to drop everything at once and go home for the funeral, because he is a business owner. On the other hand, his siblings had to ask permission from work and go through all the red tape of their respective organisations.

8. Having your own business makes you have a voice in your community as you create employment and give back to the community through social responsibility.

9. With a job, it is difficult to leave an inheritance for your children's children. Those in business can easily build businesses and create intellectual properties that will continue to pay royalties to their great-grandchildren long after they are gone from the earth.

10. Doing business and having financial intelligence gives you the financial base for a good retirement for those who want to retire. Poverty is incompatible with old age. It can be frustrating to work all your life, get to the twilight of your life, and still be working not because you want to, but because you have no choice.

11. Those who are in business have a lot of tax breaks depending on where a person lives. Whilst employees pay up to 40% of taxes depending on their pay package, entrepreneurs can always reinvest their profit into the business for expansion, and not pay any taxes in the meantime. This is one of the reasons employees are generally complaining about paying too much in taxes whilst entrepreneurs are making progress and expanding their business.

12. Entrepreneurs reduce unemployment when they create jobs for people.

FOUR REASONS WHY PEOPLE DO NOT GET INTO BUSINESS

1. **Ignorance**: A lot of people are not aware that they can do business. This lack of awareness hinders a lot a people from even thinking about it. There are many who are ignorant of how to start a business.

2. **Wrong mind-set**: A lot of people think that business is for special people with special business gifts. Some people think that to be in business you must be a crook. In Africa, some even think that everyone who is in business and doing well must be using some kind of juju or be in a secret society.

3. **Fear of Failure**: To be an entrepreneur means to take risks and be daring. To succeed in any endeavour in life, a person needs to have guts, for without the guts, there will be no glory. The main reason why the wicked servant in the parable of the talents did not invest was fear. Most people will never fulfil that which God has called them to do because of fear—fear to take risk. Most would prefer to play it as safe as possible. Life is a risk; if you do not venture, you will never gain or profit.

4. **Laziness**: Laziness is another reason why people do not get into business. People are not willing to do the work necessary to establish a business. They prefer to go to a job which they do not like for the rest of their lives. It has been said that most heart attacks occur on Monday morning as people go to jobs they do not like, to meet bosses they despise.

AND TO YOU I SAY, THIS GENERATION HAS NOT SEEN THE BEST OF YOU YET!

14

YOUR FAMILY IS YOUR FIRST BUSINESS

I believe the first business of every person is their family. The Bible says that for a person to be a leader, the person must have kids that are obedient, and be a man of one wife. So every man or woman in business should prioritize their families. Your family is the base from which you operate. If the whole world is falling apart, your house and family should be a safe haven and a place of comfort and strength.

A lot of people think that to succeed in life, ministry, or business, it means sacrificing their family. This is a lie from the pits of hell meant to frustrate the life out of a person. Many people have left their families to build empires and make money, and in the process lost their family. Then they try to use the money to win back their family. Unfortunately, sometimes the damage is almost irreparable.

He who does not take care of his own house is worse than an infidel (1 Timothy 5:8 KJV).

I have heard too many complaints from children whose fathers neglected them whilst taking care of others. Their fathers refused to pay their fees through college, but were sponsoring the kids of others. It has been said that "charity begins at home." Before we do something out of the house, we must first do it at home. We have the awesome responsibility to train our own kids first, then we can train those outside. By our own kids, I mean those in our own household, whether biological, adopted, or kids who live in our household. Some people are involved in making a name outside, to the detriment of their own families.

Whilst we should help others and give to the less fortunate, our greatest responsibility should be towards our own family first. One of the biblical criteria to be a leader in church is to be a leader first at home.

It is the responsibility of parents to train up their children the way they should go, so when they grow up they would not depart from it (Proverbs 22:6). Sometimes kids do momentarily stray, but all the lessons they learned at home bring them right back in line. It is not the responsibility of one spouse, but both parents, to raise up the child. God is not responsible for bringing up our children. We should entrust our kids to God's protection, but it is not part of God's job description to train them up. The reason we all celebrate single mothers who have raised up good and God-fearing children is because of the ginormous responsibility of bringing up children by parents, never mind a parent doing that alone. King David neglected his children and never corrected them. It is no wonder it was not difficult for one of them, Amnon, to sleep with his half-sister Tamar (2 Samuel 13:1-21). The Bible says that David had never said anything good or bad to this young man. There is no biblical record of David ever correcting Amnon and calling the family to advise them and bring reconciliation. Absalom, Tamar's brother, decided to get revenge by killing Amnon two years later. We must learn to make sure that things are working well in our house, otherwise our children can be adversely affected. No one should be ashamed or feel bad at correcting and disciplining their children with love. The purest form of love is discipline. God disciplines his children, so we should do likewise.

Eli also allowed his two sons to run rampant with all kinds of abominations in the temple, and never once brought them to correction. They both died through God's judgment and in the process, Eli died too (I Samuel 2:12-36).

Abraham, on the other hand, was an individual who took care of his family and commanded his kids to obey God (Genesis 18:19).

Some suggestions on making your family your number one business.

1. Have a family vision. Share the vision with the entire family, and tell the members of the family what role they can play to make that vision come to pass. I remember when my uncle was building a house; there were set days when everyone in the house had to pray and fast for God to make provision for the construction of the house. One of my nephews who lived with my uncle was also fasting, even at the tender age of eight. Some time later he moved to the UK to live with his mum (my elder sister). One day, his mum gave him food to eat but he refused eating— saying he was fasting. My sister was shocked, and asked him why. He said he was fasting for the building project. Do not be a mystery in your own house. Let your family know what is happening. It will be easier to achieve your goals. You will be amazed what input they can offer to expedite the fulfilment of that goal or vision.

When my dad retired as a police officer in the late '80s, he picked up a job as a contractor with an organisation called Marketing Board, in Cameroon. He was making good money until the corporation was shut down due to politics. At that time, my sister and I were in a prestigious boarding school that was expensive in terms of tuition. My mum and dad sat us down and explained to us that things were tough financially, and they could no longer afford any luxuries. They encouraged us to be content with whatever they could afford, and not compare ourselves with other kids when we went to school. Because they explained things to us, I didn't demanded much from them anymore, and would even bring home unspent pocket money from school and give it back to them.

It is also important to explain to your family the nature and demands of the business in which you are involved, at least extent they can understand. Once they know they are involved and you value their input, they will support and persevere in seasons when work might take you away from them. Once, I asked the daughter of a friend of mine who works away from home where her dad was. The five-year-old gave me a very interesting answer. She responded, demonstrating with her hands, that her dad had gone to work and would bring home a lot of money. She understood why her dad was gone for a while.

Recently, a friend of mine told me a story of a nine-year-old boy who was asking if some land that was being sold had a land title. The young man was from a tribe in Cameroon where they think business all the time. So he already understands business at such a tender age.

2. Spending time with our family. Have regular periods of spending quality time with members of the family, including spouse and children. Share dreams, fears, aspirations, etc. It creates an atmosphere of trust.
    There have been many situations, especially in Africa, where people do not know what their spouses are doing. They do not know how much they make. In fact, they know nothing about their spouses except that they are married to them. This may shock some people, but it is the plain truth.

    Go on holidays together if that is possible. If your business involves a lot of travelling, then take them along with you on some of the trips to see what you are doing, as finances permit. Maybe take just one of your kids at a time, if possible.

3. Pray and have regular sharing of the Word together. It has been said that "a family that prays together stays together." Share the vision with them. Encourage them to give ideas and input on the vision. Make them understand that they are part of the vision.
    Also, let them pray for you. I remember my uncle berating one of my cousins for not praying for him. He asked her if

she understood how his welfare is important for her survival. Many teenagers do not understand that life could be quite different for them in the absence of a caring parent.

4. Always thank and appreciate your family. Let them know how important they are to you and how they are a gift to you.

5. Teach your family to fear and love God, to be business minded, and how to develop an investment mentality. Teach them the principles of successful living, how to persevere, how to relate with people, and how to develop a biblical worldview. Teach your children to develop a reading culture. Most of these things are not being taught in schools, and it is not the duty of teachers or the latest PlayStation to bring up our kids.

AND TO YOU I SAY, THIS GENERATION HAS NOT SEEN THE BEST OF YOU YET!

15

KNOWLEDGE IN BUSINESS: THE AFRICAN ENTREPRENEUR

Whatever area of business you want to get into, it is your number one business to seek God about it. This is vitally important, since he designed you in a particular way and he knows what is best for you based on the gifts and endowments he has woven into the very fabric of your being. Business is different from investment. With investment, you can give your money to someone else to invest for you, whilst you get paid the dividends. With business, however, you are directly involved. And if you are not wired for that particular business, it can take away your peace and bring a lot of frustration and lack of fulfilment. So you have to know your primary gifts and strengths as an individual.

A man's gift maketh room for him, and bringeth him before great men (Proverbs 18:16 KJV).

You will also need to learn everything that can be learnt about your business and industry. Be diligent to know your stuff. Know what it takes to succeed in your industry, and what would give you a competitive edge. Use tools like SWOT Analysis to evaluate where you are relative to the market.

Sometimes, a person has to work for a long time for free under someone else before their gifts becomes a business. In the music industry, for instance, many people have been background singers for years before they ever go solo.

You should also have a basic understanding of the following areas.

People pay for value

The key to getting into business is creating goods or services that add value to the lives of customers. In life, you must always think of creating value. Customers do not pay money for something simply because they like the salesman. Rather, it is because what they are buying adds value to their lives or business. Therefore, if you can create a service that adds value to people, you have got a business going. The more value a good and service adds to the lives of customers, the more they will be willing to pay for it. This is just a generalization, and the very foundation of what is needed to get into business. In essence, almost everyone can create something of value.

Knowledge about money

Every businessman should know the basics of money. He should know about money cycles, and how money works. Money is called currency because it moves, or flows. That means you must understand the importance of money being invested so that it flows, else it would remain the same.

Everyone should take time to develop financial literacy. It is a great travesty not to develop knowledge and understanding about money. Money is one of the things we have to deal with on a daily basis. Money answers all things. People go to school for years to get a job that would pay them good money, yet will not take the time to learn about money. People go to work every day because they look forward to a paycheck. If money plays a great part in our everyday lives, then it is very important to understand how it works and how to manage it. Lack of financial literacy is causing a lot of heartache every day. We hear of elderly people losing their life savings to some flaky investment scheme. Sometimes this sends them to an early grave. To know how money works, buy books on finance, or even learn on the Internet. Your life will be blessed as you begin to understand how money works.

However, when it comes to financial transactions, it is very important to get the advice of financial experts.

Cash is king

In business, opportunities will come that need cash. So the person with the greatest negotiation power is generally the person who has the cash at hand. Understanding that helps you to not invest all your money in fixed assets, but to have some residual amount of money that is easily accessible when opportunities come.

Everyone should have a savings account. It is simply a wise thing to do. To be without savings means you will need a miracle all the time. The world in which we live will bring difficult situations that we never asked for, whether we like it or not. Whether we are people of faith or not, the world we live in is not a Utopia. We need to have a contingency fund.

I heard recently that the three main causes of death in America are lack of sleep, dehydration (not drinking enough water), and lack of exercise. When a person does not live a healthy lifestyle, they will most likely need medical attention down the road, or need a healing miracle. On the other hand, someone who has chosen a healthy lifestyle will generally not need a miracle. In essence, most people believe in healing but do not practice healthy living. This is also applicable in our finances. We all understand that things do happen that we have little control of, and we all need a miracle now and again in different areas in our lives. However, many emergencies in life can be avoided by having a contingency fund.

Investment mentality

Learn the investment strategies and the principles of investment. Develop knowledge about the three main pillars through which wealth is created, i.e., business, real estate, and the capital market. Money made through businesses are usually invested. As a businessman or woman, you need to know which of these investment vehicles to put your money into, so that in the long run, money can be working for you instead of you working for money for the rest of your life.

Global Mentality

Global thinking: Africans have learnt to think globally when it comes to church expansion. One of the largest Pentecostal churches in the world in terms of membership is the Redeem Church of God, having its headquarters in Nigeria. There is seldom any major city in the world—where Christianity is allowed—where a Redeem church is not found. What a blessing this is for the gospel to be propagated with such intensity.

However, when it comes to businesses, African businesses are very much lagging behind in terms of having an international or global presence. A few corporations like the Dangote Group, Zenith Bank and others are spreading their business tentacles across the continent of Africa and globally. However, I believe there are still more African businesses with more untapped potential that can become global competitors. There are still a lot of people with franchises that can go global if attention is given to such intentions. I believe it is a new dawn for African entrepreneurs who will work hard and do due diligence to transform their businesses to global entities, franchises, corporations, and conglomerates that will be floated in different stock markets.

Your network is your true net worth

When Glory and I got married, I was shocked at how many people showed up at our wedding. Even with such short notice, a lot of friends were willing to make the trip to be with us. It dawned on me that my greatest wealth is the people who truly care about me. Those that I am connected with are my real worth. At the time of our wedding, we had very little money. I was a student at the time, taking an MBA program, so my wife was the only one really working. But through the financial, material, and moral support from all the wonderful relationships we have, all we needed for our wedding was provided for and even more.

God's real wealth is in the people who are connected to him. No amount of wealth is worth a soul. God will go to any extent to see many people connected to him. He had to send his only Son to come and die on the cross to pay the penalty for humanity's sin. This was done so many could believe in Jesus and come into a relationship with him. Who you know is more important than what you know.

In every arena of life, you have to seek to be relationally wealthy. That is true wealth. At the end, all that a man really has are those he is in a relationship with. Relationship marketing has become one of the pillars in marketing. Businesses strive to keep their customers loyal by keenly attending to their interests and promptly resolving their complaints, because it generally costs far more (through advertisement) to get a new customer than to keep an existing one. Even employers know that it is sometimes better to increase the pay of existing employees and keep them, than go through the high cost of recruiting new ones.

At the moment I live in Calgary, Alberta, Canada. It is said that over 80% of jobs are gotten through networking. Only 20% or less get a job through other mediums.

AND TO YOU I SAY, THIS GENERATION HAS NOT SEEN THE BEST OF YOU YET!

16

CHARACTER IN BUSINESS: THE AFRICAN ENTREPRENEUR

A good name is rather to be chosen than great riches, and loving favour rather than silver and gold (Proverbs 22:1 KJV).

As we have seen before, to succeed in life there are two things that have to be developed: character and capacity. A person who lacks in either of these two will not do well, before God and man. The balance in these two has been an issue of great debate. I have met people, especially in religious circles, who have impeccable character, but would do nothing to develop their potential. You hear things like, "God will do it," or, "It is not about performance but about the heart." That statement is only true to a certain extent.

On the other hand, a man who develops potential without character is doomed to failure. I have seen a lot of them in the news who have committed suicide, died of an overdose of drugs, and been involved in great scandals, etc. We have all wondered what went wrong. They developed their potential without the foundation of character. We have all seen how lack of character has short-circuited their lives, and at the end they lose everything they have worked so hard for.

In Africa, where the press is less developed and where there is still a great deal of lawlessness, a lot of wealthy people can get away with "murder" as long as they have the right people in the right places.

As businesspeople, we must learn to do business with integrity, and in a way that glorifies God.

VALUES IN BUSINESS: THE AFRICAN ENTREPRENEUR

The basis on which everyone should do business is to have values.

The values of a person include his believe systems, principles, morals, and standards of behavior. Without having values, people will do anything for money, and will eventually hurt themselves. When a person has values, the person gets satisfaction in his returns, because it is not going against what he stands for.

When investing in a product, a person should not just look at the returns it brings, but what the money is being invested in, to make sure that it is in sync with what he or she stands for. For instance, a mutual fund might be investing in something that violates the human rights of others. Having that information will certainly deter a person with Christian values.

Value of Social Responsibility

There is the value of social responsibility. Most businesses now give back to the community through scholarships, food programs, etc. A lot of businesses have faced a lot of problems because they were not socially responsible to their communities. In a particular country, there has been a mass kidnapping of employees of oil companies. These companies drill oil from these communities without looking at how they can give back to these communities in the form of jobs and other amenities that can benefit the public.

Value of treating people right

In business, people are not just interested in the value of the goods and services, but also the way in which people are treated. I have sometimes gotten the worst customer service that one can imagine in Cameroon. Several times I have gone to restaurants where the service was horrendous. The staff were so rude to customers. Well, I certainly do not think it is solely the fault of the staff, but rather the responsibility of the business owners to train their staff and make them see the link between good service, reputation, and income.

There are so many stories of multimillionaires getting married to waitresses they met at restaurants—because of the great service that was offered. People sometimes tip waiters and waitresses more than the cost of the food. Serving in any form is one of the most beautiful and attractive things, and can open great doors.

Value of honesty

Most people believe that to succeed in business, one must be dishonest. The Bible says that an unjust scale is an abomination to the Lord. Anyone who does business without honesty is nothing but a scammer. To build a lasting legacy, you have to build a good name, for a good name is better than riches. Your good name can make you more money than you can imagine. Honesty, they say, is the best policy, and should be the only policy. Why not incorporate that strongly in your business and see the miles it will take you.

Value of fairness

In doing business, we should be fair and make sure that people are not being exploited. Rather than making large sums of money immediately, it is the relationship which will last for years to come that is important. Some businesses tend to overcharge their customers, especially when they don't have competitors around. Sooner or later, a substitute product may come out at a much lower price and they will lose all their business. I know of businesses that practice fairness and ensure that they do not exploit those who produce the raw materials. Sometimes, businesses do not pay their workers what is rightly due to them. To do this is setting the stage for some kind of trouble in the future.

Value of Excellence

The African entrepreneur should strive for excellence in whatever goods or services he produces. No one cares where you come from, as long as they see excellence. For a while people might not subscribe to your services for one reason or another, but when they see excellence in delivery for a long time, they will eventually change their minds and do business with you.

AND TO YOU I SAY, THIS GENERATION HAS NOT SEEN THE BEST OF YOU YET!

17

CONCLUSION

I believe the time has come for Africans to take their place in business on the global stage. To achieve this, the African must take his destiny into his hands, having God as the number one business partner. The African must have a vision that transcends three generations. This is because the least God expects of us is to leave an inheritance for our children's children. The African must study to show himself approved, a workman that does not need to be ashamed. To go into business without investing in developing the mind through rigorous and expanded reading is failure waiting to happen. The African needs to depart from old thinking patterns and renew his mind. The African must believe in himself and the potentials that God has invested in him. Finally, the African must be a giver, because living is giving.

AND TO YOU I SAY, THIS GENERATION HAS NOT SEEN THE BEST OF YOU YET!

ABOUT THE AUTHOR

Godlove Ngufor is a Pastor, teacher, investor and life coach. He believes that God has a great and unique purpose for every human being and has given every one unique potentials to help them fulfil that purpose which is part of His grand eternal plan and purpose.

Godlove also believes God expects every person to collaborate with Him to fulfil their individual purposes and attain their maximum potential.

Godlove has great ability to bring out the best in people through teaching, preaching and the books he writes. His books and teachings are laced with a lot of humor and practical life examples that are easy to understand and apply.

He is the founder of Empowering Potential Inc., a consultancy based in Calgary with the mission of helping individuals, company and institutions achieve their goals and attain their highest potentials. He holds a BSc in Microbiology and an MBA in Finance.

He is blessed with his wife Glory Ngufor and they both have been blessed with two children, Radiant and Reuel-Divine. He currently resides in Calgary, Alberta in Canada

A WORD FROM
OUR SPONSORS

Made in the USA
Charleston, SC
22 November 2014